DAVID

# LUCKY YOU

How to Get Everything You Want &
Create Your Ideal Life Using
the Law of Attraction

# LUCKY YOU

How to Get Everything You Want &
Create Your Ideal Life Using
the Law of Attraction

by

David Hooper

© 2009 KRE, LLC – All Rights Reserved

For more information on this series,
please visit us on the web at
**BoldThoughts.com**.

ISBN: 978-1-60842-003-2

KRE, LLC
PO Box 121135
Nashville, TN 37212-1135

# Contents

## Understanding The Law Of Attraction........1
**Is the Law of Attraction Real?**

## Section I
## How To Use The Law Of Attraction To Get Everything You Want ..............................21

5 Powerful Rituals for Easy Manifesting ....................23

Progressive Manifesting
*A Gradual, Step-by-step Process for Creating Your Best Life*..............................................................................42

Positive Manifesting in a Negative World ..................61

Manifesting Under Pressure
*How to Stay Focused in the Midst of Chaos and Upheaval*............................................................80

Detached Manifesting
*How to Let Go, Trust, and Believe That Your Desires Are on the Way!* .......................................99

## Section II
## 17 Ways To Attract Abundance .......................119

## Section III
## What To Do When The Law Of Attraction Isn't Working............................165

# Understanding The Law Of Attraction

## Is the Law of Attraction Real?

By now you have probably heard about this mysterious phenomenon called "The Law of Attraction," but you may have wondered if it's real. It certainly sounds too good to be true that you can "wish" for something and a big genie in the sky will hurry over to drop it into your lap, right?

You may be relieved to know that the Law of Attraction doesn't work quite like that – but it is definitely REAL and you can learn how to use it effectively in all areas of your life.

Rather than thinking of the Law of Attraction as a magical wish-machine, instead try to see it as an empowering way to deliberately guide your thoughts to create better life experiences. That doesn't mean that all of your problems (or the world's problems) will vanish instantly.

What it *does* mean is that you have much more control over your life than you've dared hope before – and with this knowledge you can not only improve your own life, but also do much more to help others.

Even if you still have doubts about whether this "law" really exists, be willing to read the following pages with an open mind. We're going to share some helpful information and examples to demonstrate exactly how the Law of Attraction works, and how easy it can be to use it in your everyday life.

## *What is the Law of Attraction?*

The Law of Attraction is often referred to as a "universal law" that determines the quality of our experiences in everyday life. The overriding concept with the Law of Attraction is "like attracts like" – which means we attract situations, experiences and people that correspond with our dominant thoughts.

For example, have you ever known a very "negative" person who always complained and spoke negatively about everything in their lives? And did you notice that that person tended to have more problems than other people did? Their problems may have ranged from troubled, rocky relationships, to career blockages, to health problems, to financial shortages and beyond.

Did they really "attract" all of that into their lives? Or were they just cursed with "bad luck"?

When you understand how the Law of Attraction works and you start paying attention so you can see it in action, it becomes very clear that each of us is 100 percent responsible for the things we experience every day of our lives.

You can probably recall many experiences in your own life in which your mindset seemed to be the deciding factor in how the situation played out. Like when you worried obsessively about something bad happening and it did happen exactly as you feared it would. Or when you wanted something so badly that you couldn't stop thinking about it and it ended up coming to you in a "miraculous" way.

## *The Law of Attraction Can be Subtle*

However, the Law of Attraction doesn't always work in obvious ways – meaning you don't have to think about a specific event in order to attract it into your life. You may be able to recall some things you worried about that didn't happen, right? And you may be able to recall plenty of things you wanted but didn't get.

The reason for those apparent anomalies is that your thoughts, feelings and beliefs were not on the same "energetic frequency" as the events, so they didn't happen. We'll be explaining how that works in more detail shortly.

For now, understand that just having your thoughts on the same energetic "frequency" as an event is enough to draw it toward you. Here are some good examples:

- Being angry at your boss can attract other people who will do things that make you feel angry.

- Being frustrated about financial problems can attract other examples of "shortage" in your life, like losing money on a deal or something valuable being stolen from you.

- Complaining that nothing ever works out for you can attract plenty more situations that don't work out.

You will attract situations that match the "energetic frequency" or your most frequent thoughts, feelings and beliefs. What does "energetic frequency" mean, exactly? Read on to learn more about exactly how the Law of Attraction works.

## How Does the Law of Attraction Work?

The Law of Attraction is activated by a "signal" or "frequency" you emit according to your thoughts, feelings and beliefs. The universe receives this "signal" like a big satellite dish, and then immediately starts returning situations, events and people that correspond with your signal.

- Positive thoughts attract positive events, experiences and people into your life.

- Negative thoughts attract negative events, experiences and people into your life.

However, this process can be a bit more complex because it's not just your thoughts that contribute to the process. Your feelings also act as a "booster" for whatever thoughts you are thinking. So, just thinking "I am a millionaire" will not instantly make you a millionaire because most likely you don't *FEEL* like a millionaire (unless you are one).

Your beliefs are also an important part of this process. Even if you think about being a millionaire, and you can somehow get into the feeling of being a millionaire, you may have beliefs that prevent your millions from arriving, such as "Money is evil; people who have a lot of money are selfish; I have to work really hard to earn money; I never have enough money to make ends meet," and so on.

Your beliefs act as a filter that allow only experiences that fit with the existing structure, and they will block anything that conflicts with them. This is one of the major reasons why people have such a hard time changing bad habits or forming better habits. In fact, let's look at an example of how habits fit into the attraction process.

## *Habits and The Law of Attraction*

Let's say that it's January 1st and you have decided that it's finally time to quit smoking and live a healthier lifestyle. Prior to this day you have prepared yourself to kick the habit and you are eager to get started. At midnight on December 31st you toss out your cigarettes, lighters and ashtrays and go to bed feeling excited about the new non-smoking you.

The next morning you wake up and immediately start thinking about smoking. The thought of being without cigarettes all day makes you feel anxious and you start to second-guess your decision to quit smoking. But, you really do want to kick the habit so you decide to put on a brave face and do your best.

As you move through your day, you start feeling irritable and nervous because you really want to smoke but you can't. In the back of your mind, you may be having thoughts like this: "I don't know if I can do this. Smoking relaxes me. How can I cope with stress if I can't smoke? My life is really stressful. How am I going to handle this until the withdrawals are gone?"

Underlying these fearful thoughts are feelings that go along with them, such as anxiety, pressure, nervousness, and uncertainty. As you radiate this fearful "signal" to the universe, you will start attracting situations that make you feel pressured, stressed, and anxious – which makes you want to smoke even more! Before long, you can't stand the pressure any longer, so you cave in and start smoking again.

Now, here's the interesting thing. If you know how the Law of Attraction works, you can actually use it to make quitting smoking (or changing any habit) effortless. Rather than allowing those fearful thoughts to start playing in your mind, you could purposely start thinking thoughts like this: "This will be a breeze. I'm strong enough to deal with any cravings I get today. A craving is just a feeling and they don't last long anyway. I choose to feel calm and peaceful all day today."

And as you focus on those thoughts consistently, corresponding emotions of peace, confidence and well-being are triggered in your body. You begin emitting a signal to the universe that all is well and the universe reflects back that reality in your surroundings.

That doesn't mean you won't experience moments of nervousness as you transition from smoker to non-smoker. But if you keep your thoughts moving in a positive, calming direction, quitting will become much easier because you will be using the Law of Attraction in a positive, proactive way – rather than allowing your thoughts to work against you.

## *How to Use the Law of Attraction Consciously*

Beyond changing your habits, you can use the Law of Attraction in many ways to make your daily life easier. It's interesting to note that most of us use the Law of Attraction in a negative way, simply because that's what we're used to doing. Have you ever said things like this when you were setting a goal or trying to accomplish something?

- "I just know this isn't going to work."
- "I'm not lucky like some people."
- "That kind of thing never works out for me."
- "No matter what I do I can't get ahead."
- "Life is hard."

When it comes to the Law of Attraction, statements like those are REQUESTS you are sending to the universe! This is a hard concept for many people to believe because it doesn't seem possible that we have that much power over our circumstances. But when you start being very deliberate about what you think and the words you say – and more importantly, the EXPECTATIONS you hold about specific situations, you begin awakening your true power as a conscious creator.

How would you start being more deliberate in what you create?

One of the easiest ways to begin is by first paying attention to the caliber of thoughts that run through your mind on a daily basis. From time to time during your normal activities, pause and turn your attention inward and consider, "What am I thinking about right now? Am I worrying about something, feeling angry about something, or otherwise focusing on negativity?" If you are indeed focused on negativity, begin turning your thoughts in a positive direction.

For example, let's say you just noticed that you're worrying about a financial problem and your body is overcome with feelings of anxiety because of it. In that moment, you have the power to change what you're thinking, which will change what you're feeling, which will change the content of your "frequency" and the universe will begin sending different experiences into your life (like increased financial abundance).

Here's an example of something you could say to help ease your feelings of anxiety: "Okay, I'm obviously worried about this problem, and worrying doesn't make me feel good. Instead I'm going to trust that it will all work out somehow. In fact, when I really think about it, things have a way of working out if I just do what I can and hope for the best."

Just saying something like that once should be enough to minimize your feelings of anxiety slightly – but the important thing is to keep saying it over and over whenever you notice that you're starting to feel anxious.

The Law of Attraction responds to your DOMINANT thoughts and feelings. Just thinking about something once isn't usually enough to attract it unless it already corresponds to related existing beliefs. Changing your outer circumstances requires a consistent, ongoing focus on the situations and events that you want to experience.

- If you want to attract more money, you must consistently focus on the thought and feeling of having plenty of money – and avoid focusing on not having enough money.

- If you want to attract the love of your life, you must consistently focus on the thought and feeling of being happy and in love – and avoid focusing on feelings of loneliness and emptiness.

- If you want to attract a better job, you must consistently focus on the thought and feeling of having a job you love – and avoid focusing on what you don't like about your current job.

It's really simple once you get the hang of it: don't focus on anything you don't want to replicate in your life, and focus all of your attention on things you DO want to receive. As simple as it seems, it can also be incredibly challenging.

How do you NOT focus on the problems, the struggles, the annoyances and the LACK of the things you want?

## *The Magnetic Nature of Thoughts*

The wonderful thing about your thoughts (and the terrible thing about your thoughts) is that they are MAGNETIC. That means one thought on a certain frequency will immediately begin attracting other thoughts that are on the same frequency.

This can be a very good thing, or a really bad thing. Think one positive thought and you've got a stream of positive thoughts moving through your mind, making you feel better and better. Think one negative thought and before you know it you're overcome with more and more negative thoughts and feelings.

Every thought triggers a corresponding feeling, and every feeling you have provides a little more "fuel" for your thoughts. The signal you radiate to the universe contains the energetic essence of these thoughts and feelings, and you start receiving situations and experiences that match them.

We've covered that already. But probably, up to now, you've been seeing evidence of this in a negative way. Now you can start using this phenomenon in very positive ways.

In our last example about financial anxiety, you saw that choosing a few more positive thoughts is enough to make you start feeling better and attracting a more positive outcome.

However, you don't always have to be in a negative situation to do this. In fact, you can get into the habit of being very proactive and apply the concept to every single aspect of your life.

The formula to remember is: thoughts, feelings, expectations, beliefs.

Ideally you want your new habit to cover each of those bases. That means not only do you want to "think a few positive thoughts" (although that is a great start) – but you also want to be aware that you can *CHOOSE* to experience virtually anything you want if you simply align your thoughts, feelings, expectations and beliefs with the desired outcome.

Let's use another example so you can see how it would work.

In fact, let's stick with the same theme for this example: financial anxiety. Let's say that that moment of financial anxiety wasn't a random thing; that you almost always feel anxious about money and you constantly struggle to pay your bills. Perhaps your job doesn't pay much, or you have accumulated a lot of debt so your income is barely enough to cover your minimum payments.

As a result, you constantly feel like a heavy weight is bearing down and you frequently feel overwhelmed by feelings of stress and anxiety relating to money and bills.

Your desired outcome is obvious: you want to pay down your debt and have more money! That can be accomplished in many ways, and you don't even have to figure out exactly how to do it yourself.

Instead, you can begin deliberately projecting your thoughts and feelings toward the outcome you want and you will trigger the Law of Attraction to begin sending the means and resources to eliminate the problem. That might mean you will be offered a better paying job, or more money might come to you in other ways, or other things will happen that you can't even imagine yet.

## *How to Deliberately Align With Your Chosen Outcome*

Since you know that your thoughts, feelings and beliefs all combine to attract the essence of the experiences in your life, and since you know that every thought you think is magnetic, how would you begin attracting better financial circumstances?

That's right, by thinking about having more money! However, it's important to realize that you have to do this from the standpoint of actually having more money, NOT wishing you had more money from the standpoint of not having enough money.

Read that sentence again, because it will make the difference between successfully attracting more money and simply attracting more financial problems.

A person who is struggling with financial problems would probably have a dominant thought pattern that goes something like this: "I never have enough money. I just can't earn enough money to get ahead. I have so many bills, how am I ever going to pay all these down? I'm so tired of being broke. I want so many things but I can never afford anything!"

Those types of thoughts simply draw more related thoughts of not having enough, which triggers corresponding emotions, which radiates a corresponding signal . . . you know the drill by now.

To turn financial struggle into financial abundance, you would have to think thoughts more like this: "I really love the feeling of having plenty of money. I can imagine what it would feel like to have all of my bills paid in full. Wow, I would love that feeling! I'd feel so free, so lighthearted. I would be able to build up a nice savings account, travel a little bit, maybe even help out some of my family and friends. That would be so great!"

And you would need to think thoughts like these over and over again every day, not just once. You need to make this thought pattern your dominant thought pattern to replace the old, negative thought pattern.

That may sound like it requires a lot of effort, and in some ways it does, but remember the good news about your thoughts being magnetic. Every one of those positive thoughts about money will begin to attract more positive thoughts about money, which will trigger positive emotions about money, which will begin to attract more money!

Now that you've got your thoughts and feelings moving into alignment with having more money, you should also pay attention to your expectations and beliefs, especially if they might be in conflict with the outcome you want.

For example, let's say you have been thinking and feeling more positively about money, but deep down inside you don't really believe that it's going to work. Somewhere in the back of your mind you might be thinking, "This is a waste of time; I'm not the kind of person who could attract more money even if it was possible; maybe it works for other people, but it probably won't work for me."

Those kinds of doubts (beliefs) will absolutely block your abundance from coming because despite the more positive thoughts and feelings you are radiating, your belief structure is communicating to the universe that you don't want to have more money. Consciously you do, but subconsciously you don't believe you can, so you won't allow yourself to receive it.

To overcome this type of internal blockage, you simply need to begin changing your beliefs about what is possible for your life, what you deserve to have and what you will allow yourself to have.

If you really don't believe that the Law of Attraction will work for you, start actively looking for evidence that it does work. Think about times in your past when you attracted something you wanted, or even times when you attracted something you didn't want because you were worrying about it. Seek out personal accounts from other people who have learned how to use the Law of Attraction in their own lives; the Internet is full of them.

As you keep focusing more and more on this kind of "evidence," little by little you will start to believe that it's possible for you to achieve the same kind of success in your own life.

Finally, get your conscious expectations working in your favor by deliberately EXPECTING more money to come to you. In the morning when you wake up, say out loud, "Today I bet some money will come to me in fun and easy ways." Or you might say, "I am open to receive some great experiences today, including more money!"

The wording doesn't matter – just that you communicate your positive expectation that money and abundance will come to you somehow, someway.

Be aware that changing a dominant pattern like this most often is not accomplished in one day. It may take weeks of consistent focus before you really start to see results, but if you stick with it day after day, two things will likely happen.

1) First, you'll start to notice that it gets easier and easier to stick with the positive thoughts as time goes on. Negative thoughts will become less and less prevalent as the positive thoughts become stronger.

2) Little by little, you'll start to see results. At first they may be very small results, like receiving a few extra dollars here and there, getting a better deal on something you had to buy anyway, and other forms of abundance coming to you easily and more frequently.

When you start seeing these things happening, be glad because it means you have started to turn the tide to better and better experiences!

## *Deliberately Choosing a Better Outcome Moment to Moment*

Now that you've seen the process in action, you should be feeling more confident about knowing how to begin improving every area of your life – just start choosing thoughts that go along with the outcome you want, allow the feelings of such an outcome to flow through your body, and believe and expect that you will get the outcome you want.

You can even use this same approach in mundane situations, not just the "problems" in your life.

For example, how about intending that your drive to work will be smooth and easy? How about affirming that an obstacle will be cleared easily so you can move forward on your goals again? How about believing that you will attract a few new clients this month? Or that your doctor will give you a clean bill of health at your checkup next week?

In every situation consider, "What type of outcome would I like to experience? What would I like to happen next?" Then choose it, expect it and let the universe handle it for you. If there are specific action steps you can take to help make it happen, go ahead and do them. Otherwise, just wait and see if you receive any "inspired actions" from the universe, or if the situation just resolves itself without any help from you.

There are endless moments every day of your life in which you can use this powerful law to bring about a wonderful outcome! Most people don't do it simply because they don't realize they can. You are no longer one of them.

## *Does the Law of Attraction Conflict With Religious Teachings?*

One major stumbling block that many people experience with the Law of Attraction is the worry that it may conflict with their religious beliefs. If you have wondered about this too, you may be pleased to know that the Law of Attraction has been mentioned (or hinted at) in many well-known religious texts, and supported by many well-respected religious and spiritual teachers through the centuries. Here are a few examples:

### Christianity

Though some Christians denounce the Law of Attraction as Satan's attempt to seduce people with material temptations, there are several biblical passages that seem to support the notion that our thoughts create our reality in one form or another.

For example, in Luke 6:38, "Give, and it will be given to you. A good measure, pressed down, shaken together and running over, will be poured into your lap. For with the measure you use, it will be measured to you." This echoes the belief "whatever you send out comes back to you" that is common in many Law of Attraction teachings.

In Proverbs 23:7 it says, "As a man thinketh in his heart, so he is" which seems to support the idea that our beliefs about ourselves and our lives will become reality.

In Matthew 9:22 it says, "Jesus turned and saw her. 'Take heart, daughter,' he said, 'your faith has healed you.' And the woman was healed from that moment." This provides another example of the power of belief (faith) and how it can alter our physical circumstances.

There are endless other examples in the Bible that seem to make the Law of Attraction and Christianity compatible.

## Buddhism

Several famous quotes by Buddha also point to correlations between the Law of Attraction and Buddhist teachings:

Buddha: "A wise man, recognizing that the world is but an illusion, does not act as if it is real, so he escapes the suffering." This supports the idea that everything around us is but a "reflection" of our dominant thoughts, feelings and beliefs.

Buddha: "All that we are is the result of what we have thought. If a man speaks or acts with an evil thought, pain follows him. If a man speaks or acts with a pure thought, happiness follows him, like a shadow that never leaves him." This one is pretty self-explanatory – we get back what we put out into the world.

Buddha: "Every human being is the author of his own health or disease." Most Law of Attraction teachings state that we are the "authors" of everything we experience, not just health or disease.

## Hinduism

Likewise, many Hindu proverbs seem to emphasize the concepts of faith and reaping what you sow that are popular in Law of Attraction teachings:

Hindu proverb: "A man becomes like those whose society he loves." (What you focus on or "love" expands.)

Hindu proverb: "A person consists of his faith. Whatever is his faith, even so is he." (You are what you believe you are.)

Hindu proverb: "There is nothing to accept, nothing to reject, nothing to dissolve." (Everything we see and experience is an illusion, reflected according to our own thoughts and beliefs.)

## *Religion, Law of Attraction and You*

In the end, no one can convince you that the Law of Attraction is real – except yourself. And no one can tell you whether it conflicts with your religious beliefs or not; only you can decide that.

However, keep in mind that Law of Attraction principles can also be adjusted to fit with almost any religious beliefs. In fact, here is a good way to look at it:

- Do your religious beliefs forbid thinking positively about yourself and the world around you?

- Do your religious beliefs forbid holding positive beliefs about yourself and others?

- Do your religious beliefs forbid you to be happy, healthy and abundant?

If you answered no to those questions, the Law of Attraction does not have to conflict with your religious beliefs. In fact, you don't have to see the Law of Attraction as a mysterious, "magical" process that supersedes your trust and faith in God, but rather as a tool that God has given to all of us to help us create our best lives possible. This benefits not only ourselves, but also everyone around us, and the entire world.

## *Is the Law of Attraction Real?*

After reading this report, do you have a stronger belief that the Law of Attraction exists? Have you been able to recall personal experiences where it seemed to be in motion? Even if you still have doubts, you can begin working with the concept little by little if you are merely willing to believe that it could be possible.

As you consistently apply the concepts to your everyday experiences and begin to see the results for yourself, your belief will grow stronger and stronger, until eventually you will have overwhelming evidence that the Law of Attraction is not only real, but also incredibly easy to use to create the life of your dreams.

# SECTION I

# HOW TO USE THE LAW OF ATTRACTION TO GET EVERYTHING YOU WANT

# 5 Powerful Rituals for Easy Manifesting

By now you probably know how to use the Law of Attraction: decide on something you want, visualize yourself having it, flow positive feelings about having it, believe it is already yours, and the universe will find a way to manifest it.

Easy, right?

Unfortunately it's not always that easy because most of us have life challenges that get in the way and ultimately block the things we want from arriving.

Some common blockages are:

**1) Stress and Frustration**

Feeling stressed and frustrated much of the time instantly creates resistance in the signal you send out to the universe. As a result, you end up attracting more and more situations in which you feel stressed and frustrated.

Worse, when you feel stressed and frustrated, you are not in energetic alignment with the things you are trying to attract, so they cannot manifest.

**2) Impatience**

Have you ever tried to manifest something that you wanted really badly and it seemed to take forever to manifest? Perhaps you are still waiting for it to manifest?

It's hard not to feel impatient when this happens, but feeling impatient can only continue to delay your manifestation because once again you are not energetically aligned with what you want.

## 3) Lack of Focus

Let's face it; it's not easy to stay focused on the great things you want when you've got so many distractions in your life (many of them quite negative and in opposition to the things you want).

How can you focus on abundance when you are burdened with debt and financial struggle? How can you attract your dream job when you are stressed to the max by your current job?

In situations like these, you end up splitting your focus randomly between what you want and what you don't want – which means you get mixed results.

These challenges may make it seem impossible to manifest the things you want, but there IS a way to overcome these challenges and develop a laser-sharp focus that will improve your ability to attract anything you desire. That way involves something that seems simple at first glance: RITUAL.

A ritual is like a ceremony that is performed regularly in the same way every time. You probably think of rituals in a religious context, but they do not have to be religious in nature.

In fact, if the word "ritual" raises negative connotations in your mind, you can just as easily refer to them as practices, processes, habits, or any other definition that fits.

Using rituals in your manifestation practice can be extremely powerful because performing a series of actions over and over again with a specific outcome in mind helps shift you into the mindset and mood you want to be in – and helps shift you OUT of the mood or mindset that you do not want to be in.

## *Shifting Your Frequency*

In other words, ritual is a great FREQUENCY SHIFTER.

What if you could, at will, shift yourself into the right mental and emotional frequency to attract the things you want? And what if you spent time doing this on a daily basis so that you were consistently emitting a strong, positive frequency related to those things you want?

The benefit is obvious: faster, more consistent manifestations.

In the following pages you will discover five easy rituals that you can use to better attract the things you want. The methods themselves are powerful because they help shift you into a better state of thought and emotion – the very states of thought and emotion that you will experience once your desires have indeed manifested.

As you know, switching your focus in this way is powerful because the universe must respond to your "request" and deliver the conditions and experiences that would give you that feeling in physical reality.

## *Consistency Counts!*

Before we get to the rituals, understand that the more consistent you can be with these rituals, the better they will work for you. If you perform them haphazardly, your results will likely be haphazard too. You do not have to perform all five rituals every day, but at least pick your favorite and do that one daily; or cycle them so you perform a different one each day. Most important is your willingness to devote the time to your manifestation practice on a regular basis.

For best results, you'll want to set aside a block of time for yourself every day, or several times a week at the minimum. All of these rituals can be completed effectively in 15 to 30 minutes, so they need not become unmanageable even if your life is very busy.

You can perform your rituals first thing in the morning, mid-afternoon, before bedtime – or any time that works best for you. However, try to stick with the same time period each day so that it becomes a habit and you're less likely to skip it.

All of these rituals can also be altered to better suit your own preferences too. Feel free to incorporate your own favorite methods so you create a ritual that you truly enjoy and get a lot of benefit from.

## *Preparing for Your Rituals*

Before each ritual, you may want to spend some time getting prepared so you can make it more "official." Treat these rituals as sacred rites; a time to reconnect to your Source and begin building a better reality – a rich, delicious reality that you deserve to have!

There are a few ways you can prepare for your rituals to enhance the experience:

- Take a ceremonial "cleansing" shower or bath before you begin. As you bathe, imagine that you are washing away all remnants of negativity that may have been clinging to you mentally, emotionally and physically. See them swirling away down the drain, leaving you feeling refreshed, invigorated and energized.

  If you like, you can also apply a few dabs of a favorite cologne, perfume or essential oil to consecrate (or devote) yourself to the upcoming ritual.

- Set the mood in the room where you will perform the ritual by playing some inspiring or calming music on low volume. Try to stick with selections without lyrics so you're not distracted by them. Some good choices might be Native American flute music, piano, harp, guitar, or even some soothing nature sounds like a babbling brook or birdsong.

- You can also light scented candles and incense to stimulate your sense of smell and create a soft glow in the room.

Most importantly, try to choose a time and place where you will not be disturbed for the next 15 to 30 minutes. If your household is very busy that may not be easy, but do your best.

A final note: You'll notice that most of these rituals involve writing in some form – but you do not have to write if you don't want to. Instead, modify the ritual slightly and perform the writing parts by speaking them out loud.

Writing them down is more effective because you'll spend more time on it and therefore "tune into" the frequency a bit better, but you will still receive some benefit from speaking aloud too.

All right, on to the rituals!

**Ritual #1 – Have it Now**

The "Have it Now" ritual will help shift you into the state of being in which you already have the things you want. Whether you are trying to attract more abundance, your dream career, your soul mate, or a slender, gorgeous body, the key to manifesting it is to feel as if you already have it!

For best results, use this ritual for only one goal at a time so you can really focus on the feeling of it. Start by spending 5 or 10 minutes with your eyes closed, breathing slowly and deeply.

Focus only on the rhythm of your breath as it moves in and out of your body.

Feel your abdomen expand, then your chest, with every inhalation, and then feel your lungs and then your abdomen deflate and relax as you exhale slowly. With each exhale, imagine that you can feel all stress and tension flowing easily out of your body, leaving you in an ever-deepening state of relaxation.

When you feel completely relaxed, take a sheet of paper and a pen and write at the top of the page:

"If I had _____ now, I would feel really . . ."

In the blank space, write the object, condition or experience you wish to have. For example: If I had a loving relationship; if I had financial freedom; if I had a slender, fit body . . .

(Remember, focus on just one thing at a time, but you can use more than one word to describe it, as in "slender, fit body" or "financial freedom and security".)

Now pause for a moment and consider how you would feel if you had this thing already. As ideas come to you, begin listing them below your statement at the top of the page. Try to use just one word to describe the feelings you would experience from having this thing, like "joyful, free, satisfied, abundant, energized," and so on.

Ideally you should have a list of five or more feelings.

Now go through each feeling on your list and write the entire statement.

Example: "If I had financial freedom now, I would feel really peaceful."

After writing the statement, say it out loud and stay with the thought for a few moments. What would it feel like to experience true peace as a result of financial freedom?

Tune into that feeling NOW. Feel waves of peace and calm flowing throughout your body, relaxing all of your muscles.

If you can't seem to connect to that feeling of peacefulness, try writing, speaking aloud, or mentally listing the reasons why financial freedom would make you feel so peaceful.

You might say, "If I had financial freedom now, I would feel really peaceful because I wouldn't have to worry about how I was going to pay the bills; I would just pay them. What a great feeling that would be, to just whip out the checkbook without a single worry that I wouldn't have enough. I would feel secure in the knowledge that I could cover any unexpected expenses. I would sleep really well knowing that my family and I are totally secure . . ."

As you speak about these things and imagine what it would feel like to experience them, you will be successfully tuning in to the energetic frequency of financial freedom.

It's important to stay with this feeling as long as you can, ideally five minutes or longer. Simply run through all of the reasons why you would feel peaceful if you had financial freedom now, and the many ways it would enhance your life experience – and try to feel it NOW.

Then move to the second feeling on the list and repeat the process, continuing to connect with the feelings of joy, abundance, excitement, and any other feeling you wrote on your list.

Note: When you first begin performing this ritual, you may find that you have a difficult time tuning in to the feelings, or staying tuned in for long. Don't let this upset you! All it means is that you are not used to the frequency and you need to keep working on it. The more you practice tuning into the new frequency, the easier it will be to stay tuned in – even when you are not actively engaged in a ritual.

In the meantime, here's another ritual to practice.

**Ritual #2 – Loving the Essence of Your Desires**

This ritual is an excellent way to begin embracing the essence of your desires, especially if you have trouble imagining what it would be like to "have them now" as we covered in the last ritual. The "essence" of your desires could also be called their energetic "frequency."

Unlike the last ritual, however, this ritual only requires that you "love" them – whether you can imagine having them or not.

This ritual also can be done verbally, though writing it down is usually more effective.

Once again start by taking a few minutes to breathe deeply and get very relaxed.

Then write at the top of a sheet of paper, "I really love the thought of _____ . . ." and fill in the blank with the desire you wish to manifest at this time.

Some examples:

- "I really love the thought of meeting Mr. [or Ms.] Right."
- "I really love the thought of living in my dream home."
- "I really love the thought of being a fit size 6."
- "I really love the thought of taking a cruise around the world."
- "I really love the thought of having a successful business."

As you write or say this statement (again, stick with one at a time) you will be tuning into the very essence of what you love about your desire. You don't have to pretend you already have it; simply spend as long as you like thinking about WHY you would love to have it.

You can again take the line of thought further by expanding on the ideas, just like you did with the last ritual. This time, however, try to focus on the reasons why you love the idea of it so much.

Here's an example of how this line of thought might go:

"I really love the thought of meeting Mr. [or Ms.] Right. It would be neat to have a companion to share my life with, especially if this person was perfectly suited to me. We would probably share the same tastes in music and movies, and enjoy the same kind of activities. I love the idea of having fun with him/her, and really connecting mentally, emotionally and physically. Thinking about this feels so real to me, like it really could manifest at any moment."

Just keep going and allow your thoughts to wander where they may, all the while enjoying the little "fantasy" you are weaving about your future relationship. Rather than mere fantasy, you are actually tuning into a frequency that will begin drawing forth the connected relationship you are focusing on!

Once again, try to devote at least five or 10 minutes to this portion of the ritual (plus the time it takes to make preparations and spend a few minutes getting very relaxed).

This type of ritual can even be done "informally" when you're engaged in other routine activities during the day and evening; like when you're driving, waiting for an appointment, eating a meal, showering, or shopping.

Simply call to mind something you want, and then mentally or verbally recite the reasons why you love it and the ways it would change your life for the better when you have manifested it.

**Ritual #3 – Opening to the Flow of Abundance**

This next ritual is a little more generalized because you don't have to have a specific desire in mind to use it. In fact, of all the rituals shared here, this one is the most effective at drawing ALL good things into your life.

Once again, start the ritual with your chosen preparations, then spend several minutes breathing deeply and getting nice and relaxed.

Then say aloud, "I now open to the universal flow of abundance and allow it to flow through me and every area of my life."

Close your eyes and imagine that you are looking up toward the sky, where a large stream of brilliant light is flowing down from the heavens toward you. You can make this light any color you like, perhaps a color you would relate to abundance like green, gold, or dazzling white.

Imagine that this large stream of abundance flows over and through you, infusing every cell, organ and fiber of your being with the essence of abundance. Feel it coursing through your veins, filling you completely with light, warmth and energy.

Feel it spreading beyond your physical body to illuminate your home, your neighborhood, your vehicle, your workplace, and even your friends and loved ones.

Imagine this energy flowing effortlessly into every crack and crevice of your life, instantly cleansing and transforming negativity and lack into rampant, vibrant abundance.

If there are specific areas of your life you wish to heal, like financial problems, health problems or relationship problems, call to mind an image of these situations one by one and see them being washed gently by this loving, healing light.

See the light dissolving all turmoil, stagnation, lack, and struggle. Take a few slow, deep breaths and imagine that you are inhaling this beautiful light and allowing it to flow through your body again and again. Try to stay with these images for a minimum of five or 10 minutes.

This ritual can also be done at other times besides your scheduled ritual time, like right before you go to sleep, or during a stressful moment during the course of your day.

Simply slip away to a quiet place and spend a few moments imagining the beautiful, healing light of abundance flowing to and through you, washing away anything unwanted.

**Ritual #4 – Gratitude, Now and Then**

You may already be aware of the power of gratitude when it comes to the Law of Attraction, but this ritual puts a slightly different spin on it.

Once again start by preparing and getting relaxed. Then write (or speak) the following:

> "I am so grateful that I'm going to receive _____."

Fill in your desire in the blank space, and then begin listing the reasons why you feel so grateful that this wonderful thing is coming to you.

However, do this from the mind-set of believing with full faith that it's already yours, and it's already on the way to you.

A good example of this would be if you had won a brand-new car but hadn't yet gone to pick it up. In the days before you retrieved it you would be feeling incredibly grateful for your good fortune, and you'd be imagining how great it was going to be to go pick up your new car and enjoy driving around in it.

Take the same approach to anything else you are trying to manifest; feel grateful that it's "yours" even though it is not yet physically in your life.

You can also expand on the thoughts, like we've covered in the other rituals:

"I am so grateful that I'm going to receive a higher income. It will certainly make it easier for me to pay the bills and put food on the table; maybe even afford a nice vacation. A bigger income means greater peace of mind and I'm so grateful that I'll have that. I work hard and I deserve to be well-compensated for what I do. I'm so grateful to have a job that pays so well!"

Even if you don't know how your increased income will come, you could say:

"I know that the universe is always working on my behalf, and I'm so grateful for that! I have no idea how my higher income will come, but I do believe it will, and soon. I feel really grateful for it even though it's not quite here yet. Thank you universe, for always guiding me to my highest good!"

Obviously, the most important thing while saying or writing these things is to really FEEL grateful for the good fortune coming your way soon.

Once you have spent five minutes or so on this part of the ritual, switch your focus back to the present moment and do the same thing with your current situation.

For example:

"Even before more income comes to me, I do feel grateful for the income I already have. It may not be the highest income in the world, but it does provide a decent level of comfort for me. I'm able to keep a roof over my head and that's definitely something to be grateful for. I don't know what I would do without that paycheck! Thank you universe, for my existing income; I'm truly grateful for all I have right now."

Spend a few minutes feeling genuinely grateful and also affirming that things are only going to get better for you from this moment on.

**Ritual #5 – Releasing Control to the Universe**

This ritual is best used during those times when you feel incredibly frustrated that things don't seem to be working in your favor. If you have been trying and trying to manifest something and it just doesn't seem to be working, or if your results seem sporadic – or even if you're just having "one of those days" where you're ready to tear your hair out in frustration – this ritual can help ease your angst and replace it with inner peace.

Spend a few minutes breathing deeply and getting very relaxed, just like you do before the other rituals.

Call to mind the situation that has you feeling frustrated, hold both of your hands in front of you and close them tightly into fists. Squeeze them as tightly as you can, as if you were desperately grasping something with both hands.

Hold that pose for a few moments as you say out loud, "I don't want to let go of this. I can't let go of this. I need this situation to go my way and I'm not willing to let go!!" Put a lot of conviction and passion in your voice and stay with this sensation of desperately grasping something.

If you are feeling frustrated in general and not from a specific issue, you might change the recitation to be more like this: "I'm feeling so frustrated today! Everything is going wrong, I feel so stressed and I don't know what to do about it. I'm trying so hard to make my life better and less stressful but it's just not working!"

Either way, stay with this feeling of tension in your hands, arms and emotions – take a slow, deep breath in, pause for a moment – and then simply LET GO.

Open your hands, exhale the breath you are holding and allow your entire body to go limp.

Pause a moment, then take another slow, deep breath in and once again exhale and feel every fiber of your being letting go and becoming very relaxed.

Say out loud, "Universe, I am letting go of this situation now. [Or "this frustration now" if that's what you're currently focused on.] I have been trying desperately to control this situation and I see that it's only causing more problems. I believe that you can handle this situation much better than I can, and I believe that you can create a wonderful outcome for me, so I am turning it over to you and LETTING GO right now."

Really mean those words as you say them. Genuinely detach from your feeling of "needing" things to be a certain way in this moment, and simply surrender to what is.

As you do so, do not allow yourself to feel resigned about it! In other words, do not hold the attitude of, "This is obviously never going to happen for me, so I give up."

Instead, do this from an attitude of true peace and trust, as if you were emotionally saying, "All is well, and I know that this thing will happen for me when the time is right. Until then, I'm very willing to wait because I know that the universe is already working on it. It's okay to let go and let it all come effortlessly."

Spend as long as necessary in this state of emotional detachment, and allow feelings of peace and surrender to flow over and through you. If you do it right, you should feel like a huge weight has been lifted off of your shoulders and you should have a deep inner knowing that all is well – despite how things may appear in your outer surroundings.

Even after you finish this ritual, you may find that you occasionally slip back into your former state of frustration. When that happens, simply repeat this ritual – or better yet, do it routinely every day and make it a habit to keep "letting go" and allowing the universe to work on your behalf. The more you do it, the easier it becomes to keep doing it.

## *The Benefits of Ritual*

These rituals are very simple in some ways, but hopefully you can see the potential they hold for helping you gain control over your thoughts, feelings and intentions, and begin manifesting much more easily and consistently.

When done on a regular basis, rituals can help you to:

- **Refocus your mind.**

   Your thoughts often resemble an audio recording that keeps playing the same information over and over again, and unfortunately most often that information is negative in nature. Messages like, "I can't do this; I'm worthless; I don't deserve to be happy; I'm a failure; I can't do anything right" constantly hold you back from living your best life.

   Ritual can help you interrupt that playback and begin recording much more empowering messages like, "I trust the universe; the universe loves me and wants me to be happy; I can manifest anything I want simply by focusing on it!"

- **Reconnect you with your Source.**

   Your "Source" could be called your inner being, higher self, inner wisdom, spirit, or many other names, but it's the part of you that is infinitely wise, loving and always connected to the Divine. When you deliberately reconnect with this part of yourself on a regular basis, everything in your life seems to flow much more easily. You find yourself being led to the best opportunities, the best experiences, and a most joyful life in every way.

The key is to see these rituals as opportunities rather than chores. See them as powerful tools you have at your disposal in every situation and be committed to using them regularly to get the most benefit from them.

# Progressive Manifesting

*A Gradual, Step-by-Step Process
for Creating Your Best Life*

Once you understand how the Law of Attraction works, it seems like such a simple thing to manifest the life of your dreams. Visualize the great things you want, bring yourself into energetic alignment with them, and they manifest in your life.

You have probably seen this process in action so you know it works – but there are also a few ways it can go wrong so that it seems not to work right. Then the manifestations don't happen at all, or if you *do* make progress, it seems agonizingly slow and difficult.

One major cause of "roadblocks" like these is trying to make too much progress, too quickly.

For example, trying to jump straight from serious financial blockages to overnight millionaire; or trying to tackle many large areas at once, like attracting your soul mate while also creating your dream career with a million-dollar-a-year salary, while also dropping 50 pounds and manifesting the gorgeous body you have always wanted.

Each and every one of these dreams can be manifested; there is no question about it.

However, trying to undertake such a dramatic transformation in a short period of time is a sure route to frustration and disappointment.

As a result, most of the people who try this inevitably struggle along for a few months and finally give up altogether. These are also the people who later proclaim, "I tried using the Law of Attraction and it just didn't work for me!"

Are you one of these people? Have you had some manifesting success, but not as much as you'd like? Are you still struggling to manifest the bigger things you want?

If so, read on for a much easier way to manifest your dreams that virtually eliminates the possibility of frustration and doubt.

## *Progressive Manifesting – Small Steps Up the Energetic Scale*

Most of the frustration experienced by Law of Attraction practitioners could be avoided if they did just one thing differently: TAKE SMALLER STEPS!

Rather than trying to wave a magic wand and dramatically transform their entire lives in one fell swoop, they would have much better results if they took it one step at a time and worked on smaller, more manageable changes first.

There are several reasons why a gradual approach makes sense:

### 1) Manifesting something small seems easier.

The truth is, it takes the same amount of energy to manifest something really big as it does to manifest something small – but most of us do not really believe that. We have come to equate "bigger" with "more difficult." Therefore, when we attempt to manifest something really big and wondrous, it seems much more intimidating than it would if we started smaller.

Remember that your beliefs play a very big role in the manifestation process, so believing that something will be difficult is a sure way to make it difficult. On the other hand, when you believe something will be easy, it usually is!

## 2) We are less attached to smaller manifestations.

When we attempt to manifest something really big, we feel like we have a lot riding on the outcome – especially if we feel stressed about our current situation. Therefore we get very attached to "needing" things to be different, which creates a bunch of resistance, which slows down our ability to manifest anything good.

With smaller manifestations, it's not such a big deal if they don't work out. It doesn't seem like the end of the world for us, so we are able to relax and have fun with the manifestation process – which, ironically, usually results in much easier, faster manifestations.

## 3) We can easily build on our past success.

Seeing more frequent successful manifestations in your life – even if they are small ones – immediately makes you feel more confident in your abilities as a deliberate creator.

You know that if you were able to manifest a positive solution to a minor problem, you can probably take the same steps to manifest bigger life changes. And suddenly, those bigger life changes don't seem so intimidating anymore.

## *A Cup of Coffee and a Parking Space*

Undoubtedly you have heard the common suggestion to start small by manifesting a cup of coffee or a parking space at the mall, and these are definitely easy ways to get started.

But there are literally *thousands* of other simple ways to use the Law of Attraction that can build your confidence and help you gradually and easily master the art of manifestation. This guide is going to share many such examples so you can transform yourself into the happy, successful deliberate creator you always knew you could be.

Before we get to those, I want to make it clear that "progressive manifesting" does not mean that you can't have bigger goals. You don't have to give up the inner vision you hold for your life.

Those big dreams in your heart are there for a reason and they are not beyond your reach – but they will most likely be long-term goals, not overnight manifestations.

Continue to focus on those dreams; visualize them; create a vision board with photos that inspire you; write about them in your journal – do all of the things you were already doing to try to draw them into your life.

But at the same time start focusing more on the smaller daily manifestations that could make your life easier right now – today.

What do you need? Which challenges are you facing right now that could use quick resolutions?

These situations are perfect places to start with the power of progressive manifesting.

## *First Things First – The Cornerstone of All Successful Manifestations*

You have probably heard it a thousand times by now – feeling good is vital to the manifestation process. But many people misunderstand this concept and therefore fail to apply it beneficially.

### What is your dominant mood?

When it comes to your everyday attitude, are you more apt to sing and laugh or grumble and complain? Are you frequently relaxed and happy, or tense and frustrated?

Your "default" mood and mind-set each day has a major impact on your ability to manifest the things you want (big and small), simply because you are only able to manifest things that you are energetically aligned with receiving. Your thoughts and emotions determine your energetic "signal" and the Law of Attraction responds to this signal by returning corresponding situations into your life.

Trying to manifest great stuff when you're always in a foul mood just won't work! In order to receive positive experiences and events, you have to be in a positive state of mind and emotion.

Unfortunately, some people try to fix the problem by "faking it" – pretending that they feel good while actually still feeling fearful, angry or frustrated inside. That does not alter their energetic signal, so they keep getting experiences that make them feel even more fearful, angry or frustrated – which makes it even more difficult to feel good!

There are a few things you can do if this has been your experience so far:

### 1) Stop "trying" to feel good.

Rather than trying to force yourself to feel good to help your manifestations, try instead setting aside a block of time every day to do things that genuinely make you feel good. If you love to window-shop, make time for window-shopping! If you love to sit quietly in a park and daydream, do it! If you have a favorite hobby, engage in it as often as you can.

Make a list of all the things you truly LOVE to do – those things that make your heart sing – and then make it a high priority to do them regularly. If you worry that this may take a lot of time that you don't have, simply do them in smaller blocks of time. Ideally, try to fit in several periods of feel-good time each day, even if they are only for 10 minutes at a time.

## 2) Practice regular stress management.

Like most people, you may have a fairly stressful life (or even a very stressful one), which can block all of the wonderful things you have been trying to attract. When you feel stressed, you can only attract more experiences that make you feel stressed.

Recognizing that you're stressed isn't always so easy because it often has a way of sneaking up on you. It can seem that one minute you feel fine and the next you are overwhelmed and aggravated. Worse, it's possible to live for years in a state of ongoing stress so that it feels almost "normal" to be constantly on edge. Needless to say, this mental and emotional stress is not good for your manifestation efforts.

Here are some easy ways to help reduce and better manage stress:

### Meditation

Meditation is undoubtedly one of the simplest ways to relax your mind and body, and it can be done in short segments to easily fit with even the busiest schedule. Find a secluded, quiet place to relax, close your eyes and breathe slowly and deeply for 10 or 15 minutes. Try to quiet your thoughts and focus only on your breathing, and with every breath allow your body to feel more and more relaxed. Do this once or twice a day (or more) and you'll instantly notice how much calmer you feel.

## Downtime

How often do you give yourself permission to just relax? For stress management purposes, this should be done at least once a day, even if it's only for an hour or so. Give yourself permission to set aside all obligations and do something just for you. You can read, watch television (ideally positive programs), take a soothing bath, go for a walk, etc. Periods of downtime are a great way to let go of stress, quiet your mind, rest your body, and build up your energy and vitality again.

## Deep breathing

Deep breathing can be done while meditating, of course, but it can also be done any time you feel tense or pressured. Try taking a few slow, deep breaths while standing in line at the store; driving; working – dozens of times a day you can easily pause and let go of stress. As you do, you instantly raise your energetic frequency so you are more receptive to the things you want to allow into your life.

## Self-Talk

The things you say to yourself on a regular basis also have a dramatic impact on how stressed or calm you feel. Do you ever say things like this to yourself? "That was a stupid thing to say. Why do things always go wrong for me? Why can't I get this right?"

Negative self-talk only moves you further away from the things you are trying to attract, and keeps you feeling stressed and unhappy. Begin adopting a more positive monologue and notice how much better it makes you feel. Say things like this: "I'm getting better at this every day. I'm proud of myself for coming this far. I can handle this, no problem."

All of these techniques are important tools in your manifestation toolbox because the better you feel, the easier you will be able to attract the things you want.

### 3) Choosing daily to feel happy.

Finally, feeling good is largely dependent upon how happy you choose to feel each day. Most of us are usually in "default" mode when it comes to our mood and mind-set, and we let our outer circumstances determine how we feel. If things are going well for us, we feel happy. If things don't seem to be working out, we feel unhappy.

What we fail to realize is that by choosing to feel happy no matter what, we instantly begin attracting more and more situations in which we will continue to feel happy!

Every day when you wake up, make a strong decision to feel happy. Say to yourself, "Even if things are less than perfect in my life today, I'm going to feel happy. I'm going to make the best of everything and be optimistic that even better things are on the way."

If you notice that you're starting to feel less than happy, renew your commitment to happiness – do it dozens of times a day if you have to. Little by little, you will shift your default attitude from negative to positive.

When you truly master your thoughts and feelings and deliberately feel good as often as possible, you will notice a dramatic improvement in your ability to attract great experiences.

However, don't try to be "perfect" at this. No one is. Instead, just pay attention to how you feel throughout the day, and notice if you start to slip back into a negative focus. If you do, use one or more of the methods we've covered here and gradually shift back into a positive space. The more you work on it, the better you'll get at it – and the more efficiently you will be able to manifest both big and small goals. Let's go into some of those smaller goals now.

## Creating Small, Frequent Manifestations

We have explored the problems that result from attempting dramatic, overnight transformations, and the benefits of taking a more gradual approach. We've also gone over several effective ways to help you relax, reduce stress and feel good to allow better circumstances into your life.

Now let's look at some easy, fun ways you can start creating small, frequent manifestations and gradually build up to bigger ones.

## Partnering with the Universe

The first thing you may want to do is affirm (or reaffirm) your commitment to working with the universe, rather than trying to force everything to happen on your own. This is especially important if you are just getting started with the Law of Attraction – or if you have been struggling to make progress for any length of time.

One of the best ways to do this is by writing or speaking your intentions aloud.

Here's an example of how you might word your intention: "Universe, I am affirming my commitment to work with you as a deliberate creator every day. I ask you to please assist me in creating better conditions in every area of my life. Help me by alerting me to potential blockages, bringing opportunities to my attention, and leading me step by step in creating my goals both small and big."

Then ask the universe to send you a "sign" that your request has been received. Try to choose a specific and unusual object that you wouldn't normally see often, like a rainbow, a particular species of bird, a butterfly, a blue paperclip, or something significant to you personally. See this object clearly in your mind and spend a few minutes visualizing it.

Asking for this sign is not so the universe can "prove" anything to you; it is to help you begin building a belief that you are indeed creating your reality moment to moment.

For the next several days, recite or re-read your intention again morning and night, and spend a few minutes visualizing the object you wish to receive as a sign. However, don't obsess over the sign. Go about your normal routine like usual and allow the sign to appear when the time is right. Most often it will come in a way that is totally unexpected and fun.

You can also use this "send me a sign" method when you are seeking guidance on a specific problem or situation, or when you're trying to make a decision on something important, etc.

**Setting Daily Intentions**

Another great way to get into the habit of manifesting small things daily is to set an intention for each day when you first wake up.

You can do this in two ways:

> **1) General intentions.**
>
> You can say something like, "I intend that today is filled with great experiences in every way. All good things flow easily to me today, including money, interesting people, great opportunities and goodness in all forms."
>
> **2) Specific intentions.**
>
> You can also set intentions for more specific issues: "I intend that the perfect solution for [state your situation] comes to me today. Universe, I know you will lead me and guide me to the perfect solution and I will do my part by staying alert for signs and hunches I receive."

The best thing about this daily intention activity is that the more you do it, the stronger your belief will grow that the universe is indeed hearing your requests and answering them – which will lend that much more power to your future intentions and make them work even better.

**Manifesting Today's Needs**

When people try to manifest really huge goals, it's usually because they're trying to create better conditions for the rest of their lives. A common example is when a person tries to win millions in the lottery so they'll never have to worry about money again. They don't need millions right now, but they believe it would make them feel more secure to have it "just in case."

Unfortunately, it can take a very long time to get into alignment with millions of dollars, especially if you're currently dealing with a lot of financial problems. Rather than trying to manifest a few million overnight, a much easier approach is to instead consider how much money you need right now, <u>today</u> (or even this month).

Do you have a bill for $100 that needs to be paid? Ask for that much money to come to you! Say to the universe, "I have this bill for $100 that needs to be paid; please send me the funds to pay it quickly. If there is anything I can do to help manifest the money, please let me know. Otherwise I know that the money will come to me easily. Thank you."

In fact, you can do this every month with all of your expenses. Put them all together in a pile, add up the total, and have a talk with the universe. Say, "Universe, here are my bills for this month, totaling $2,487.00. I know for sure I will have $2,000.00 coming in, but I will need a bit more than that. Please show me a way to obtain more money, or simply let it flow to me in fun and easy ways. Thank you."

Then – be sure not to worry about money from that point on. If you worry "How am I going to pay these bills?" you will block money from coming to you. Instead, keep affirming that the universe is working on it, and you will have the money to pay the bills easily.

This same method can be used for anything you need; a job, a solution to a problem, a vehicle, healing, and more – whatever you most need each day, ask for it. Be optimistic, believe that your solution is coming, and expect the situation to be resolved quickly and easily.

Then, be sure to listen to your inner guidance throughout the day. If you feel an urge to go to a specific place or call someone, do it. You just might be led to the perfect solution.

It's amazing how quickly you can see results with this method – and the more firmly you believe it will work, the better it does work. Solutions can often appear almost before you have time to recognize that there is a problem!

**Making Bad Situations Better**

Another great way to create some easy manifestations is to be proactive in making bad situations better. For example, imagine that you went to work one day and found that your boss was in a terrible mood, barking at everyone and generally driving down the workplace morale.

When faced with a negative situation like that, most people would go along with the flow of negativity and end up in terrible moods themselves. But you don't have to. Instead, you can choose to focus your thoughts and intentions in a more positive direction and actually influence events.

Slip away to a quiet place (perhaps the restroom) for a few moments and state an intention: "I intend that my boss releases his/her anger and hostility and begins feeling happier and more positive starting now." Then close your eyes and imagine your boss doing just that. See him or her laughing and joking around, being supportive and understanding, and so on.

If you can actually remember times when your boss did behave this way, even better! Focus on those memories and firmly intend that he or she adopt this attitude right now. Then release it to the universe.

Complete the intention by stating one for yourself too: "I intend that my mood remains high and positive today, no matter what else is happening around me. I choose to feel good, to feel happy, and to easily handle anything that comes my way."

It's surprising how often this works – even when intending that other people's behavior changes. More often than not, you are not really "controlling" what they do; rather you are altering your own <u>perception</u> of them and seeing what you expect and intend to see. And if their behavior doesn't change, you have at least intended to control your own mood and mind-set, so negative behavior by others won't affect you as much as it otherwise would have.

## Replace Worry With Conviction

If you tend to worry a lot, this activity will be extremely helpful to you. Most people don't realize it, but worrying is one of the worst things you can ever do because you are actually attracting exactly what you worry about. What a destructive way to use the Law of Attraction, right?

Eliminating worry from your life is another excellent way to use the Law of Attraction to manifest on a small scale – but there are obvious, huge benefits to doing so. Rather than attracting the things you worry about, you can get into the habit of deliberately choosing what you want and stating it with conviction.

Take a moment right now to think about the types of things you worry about. Do you worry incessantly about money, your children, your spouse, family and friends, your health, the economy?

No matter the subject of your worries, start paying closer attention to your thoughts all day long, and when you catch yourself starting to worry, STOP and say something to counteract the negative thoughts and choose something better.

Here's an example:

You catch yourself thinking worrisome thoughts like this: "I hope my company doesn't start laying people off. Business has been slowing down for months, and that can't be a good sign. I really need my job right now, and so does everyone else . . ." If you stay with this line of thinking for too long, you will continually imagine losing your job and all kinds of terrible things happening as a result.

As soon as you become aware of these thoughts, stop and deliberately choose something better. Say, "Wait, that's not what I want to happen. I CHOOSE to keep my job. I INTEND that my company prospers, and all of us are given raises and bonuses. I know that all is well, and there is nothing to worry about."

You can word it more specifically to fit your situation; the important thing is to be very firm and decisive about what you want to happen, and then intend that it be so. Don't worry about how or when – leave all of that up to the universe. Your only job is to express what you want, and then expect it to happen.

Any kind of worry can be transformed into faith and conviction using this method – and once you do it a few times you'll see how well it works!

## *Working Your Way Up to Bigger Manifestations*

As you begin to master the techniques we just covered, your outer circumstances should slowly but surely begin transforming into better and better circumstances. These small changes may not seem as exciting as huge manifestations – but you sure do come to appreciate them as they happen more and more frequently.

The process also becomes easier because rather than trying to manifest something positive while surrounded by negativity, you will begin manifesting something even better while already surrounded by positive circumstances.

For example, once you have consistently manifested enough

money to cover your bills each month, then you can begin manifesting "more than enough" money, then "much more than enough" . . . and keep going until you have reached the level of abundance you want.

Same thing with your relationships; simply choose one thing you would like to improve, then another, and another, until your relationships are joyful and satisfying.

Same thing with your health, your career, your social activities – every area of your life can be transformed if you simply choose better thoughts, intend a better outcome, and get your beliefs and expectations aligned with that outcome.

The methods we have covered in this guide can be used no matter where you are starting from, and no matter how far along the path you may have already traveled.

## Patience and Detachment

With any and all manifestations you attempt, it's crucial to remember to be patient and detached from the outcome. Intend the outcome you want, believe it will happen – but don't get stuck on "needing" it to happen. The moment you become emotionally attached to anything, you are creating energetic resistance to it.

Instead, be relaxed about when and how your manifestations arrive. Don't try to force them to happen in specific ways, and don't try to push them to happen in certain timeframes. You can <u>request</u> a specific timeframe, however. For example, if you needed to pay a bill by a certain date, there's nothing wrong with asking for the money to come by that date.

But never get angry or upset if a manifestation doesn't come by a requested date. Simply affirm that there must be a good reason, the universe is still working on it and it will arrive shortly.

You can also ask the universe to show you if there is anything you can do to bring forth the desired outcome more quickly. Meditation provides a great opportunity to do this; think about a specific situation, ask for inspired guidance, then pause for a few minutes and take note of any insights or ideas that come to you. If none do immediately, they may still show up at a later time.

## *Ongoing Growth and Expansion*

In all areas of your life and in every situation you encounter each day you can be a conscious, empowered, deliberate creator and CHOOSE what you want to experience. The only challenge is learning how to control your thoughts to focus on what you want, rather than what you don't want. Once you have mastered that, there's no end to the wonderful life experiences you can create.

# Positive Manifesting in a Negative World

One of the major challenges that you may face as a deliberate creator is frequent negativity and criticism from the people in your life. Rude strangers, pessimistic loved ones, critical spouses – we all have to deal with negative people in one form or another.

When you're trying to manifest better experiences and you understand the importance of keeping your thoughts focused in a positive direction, it can seem like a futile undertaking if you're surrounded by negative people at every turn.

Your first response might be to feel angry and resentful that these people are "preventing you" from manifesting your best life – but in this guide you'll learn that you and only you are in control of manifesting your success.

You may not be able to control what other people say and do, but you are definitely in control of your responses to them.

Even better, you'll learn some effective techniques that you can use to immediately feel more in control and overcome any negative influences you may encounter in your daily life.

## *Dealing with Negativity, Criticism and Conflicting Desires*

You may have heard it said before that no one can create in your reality and you cannot create in theirs, but this certainly seems untrue when your life experiences are so deeply entwined with those of other people.

How can you manifest your dream life when your spouse wants something totally different? How can you effectively change your language from negative to positive when your best friend keeps making fun of your "dumb affirmations" or "new age mumbo jumbo"?

As you know, staying focused on what you WANT (rather than what you don't want) is crucial in manifestation – but when you are faced with dozens of sources of negativity in your everyday life, that begins to seem almost impossible to do.

There are different types of negative people, but you will probably encounter people like these most of the time:

**1) Generally negative people.**

These are the "complainers" and "victims" that feel like the world is against them. Almost every word out of their mouths is negative in some form, and no matter what you say to try to cheer them up, they will find a way to stay miserable anyway.

Worse, they can't stand it if you seem to be happy (or even in a good mood). If you speak about your goals and dreams, they will give you plenty of reasons why you can't possibly achieve them. Their goal is to keep you and everyone else feeling miserable and stuck – not because they don't love you or because they want you to suffer, but because they don't want to suffer alone. Their insecurities and fears are what keep them focused on the negative, and your positive attitude seems like a threat to them. They may even think they are "helping you" by not letting you get your hopes up and be disappointed later.

## 2) Doubters and disbelievers.

Doubters and disbelievers usually have a very cynical view of life. They are never hopeful, always pessimistic. Even when something good happens to them, they find a way to put a negative spin on it.

And they will do the very same thing to your hopes and dreams. If they notice that you are taking steps to improve your life, they'll come up with endless doom and gloom predictions that make your dreams begin to seem childish, dumb and a big waste of time.

## 3) Criticizers.

In the eyes of a criticizer, nothing is ever right. You cannot do anything right, nothing and no one can measure up to their standards, and they are sure to let you know about it at every possible opportunity.

Criticizers will point out everything wrong with your dreams, your goals, your lifestyle, your personality and more. They will point out all of your flaws and weaknesses and explain why those negative attributes will prevent you from improving your life in any way.

Criticizers may seem to be cruel and unfeeling, but they are often just as hard on themselves as they are on everyone else. Deep down inside they may struggle with strong insecurities and in an effort to compensate they allow their egos to become over-inflated and try to portray themselves as being "perfect."

It's important to point out that most of the negative people you encounter in your daily life are not being negative on purpose. They are not "evil" or "bad" in any way – they have simply developed a chronic habit of negative thinking and they can't understand why you would want to improve your thinking or your life.

Even if you can sympathize with the reasons behind their negativity, dealing with these people is not easy – in fact it can be downright exasperating at times! But if you want to manifest a better life for yourself, you will need to learn how to deal with negativity, whether it comes from other people or your own thoughts.

**Differences Are Not Always "Negativity"**

Sometimes you may be tempted to label another person "negative" because they have opinions, beliefs and preferences that differ from yours. A good example of this is a spouse who gets upset when you talk about your dream of taking a trip around the world – because he or she hates to travel and the thought of traveling around the world makes him/her feel uncomfortable.

The way your spouse expresses his or her feelings may indeed seem negative if it conflicts with your own feelings –

but this is different than a person who is always putting you and your dreams down, endlessly complaining or criticizing.

Another example of differences would be a person who wants the same outcome that you do, like your boss wanting your workflow to be smooth and productive – but he or she has different ideas about how and when it should be accomplished.

These differences are not such a big deal when they involve people you don't interact with much, like co-workers or acquaintances. But what about when it's your spouse, child, or business partner? You can't both manifest what you want because the two visions conflict with each other, right? Not necessarily!

You'll learn more about how to co-create harmoniously with spouses and life partners a bit later in this guide. For now, understand that there are endless ways that the universe can make BOTH of you happy, even if you seem to have different goals.

In the meantime, let's go over some simple strategies for taking back your power as a conscious creator so that you will be free to manifest the life of your dreams – despite any negativity that comes your way from other people.

**Taking Back Your Power**

Taking back your power as a conscious creator requires gaining control of your focus, which of course starts with your thoughts. However, this goes way beyond "positive thinking."

Later in this guide you'll learn some good negativity-neutralizing techniques, but before you can master those you really need to know how to consistently strengthen and control your focus – because the techniques require a bit of mental control themselves, and also because they are only as powerful as you believe them to be.

Your thoughts are your greatest power when using the Law of Attraction. Energetically speaking, not having good mental control is like waving a loaded gun around, shooting randomly at whatever happens to be in the way. Your thoughts also "fire" whenever you focus on something, but instead of blowing a hole in the object, you actually begin attracting more of it into your life.

Positive thinking techniques like affirmations, visualization and purposeful optimism are all good ways to begin reigning in control of your thoughts and placing your focus on something better, but that's just the tip of the iceberg.

**Watch What You Feed Your Mind**

Do you frequently watch or listen to negative programming on television, radio or the Internet? Do you get drawn into heated arguments with friends and associates – or even in Internet chat rooms, discussion forums or blogs?

These negative activities will absolutely keep drawing more negativity into your life. You may end up attracting more negative people (or more encounters with the existing negative people in your life), or you may attract more negative experiences, challenges and obstacles simply because you are focusing on negativity so often.

Successfully controlling your thoughts requires you to think carefully about the things you give your attention to and ask yourself, "Is this something I would like to see more of in my life?" If the answer is no, then you need to be committed enough to turn your attention away from it and focus on something better.

Doing this consistently takes determination, but the effort is well worth it.

**Avoiding Taking on Other People's Moods**

Other people's negative moods can absolutely affect your own mood if you're not careful. Later you'll learn some good preventative exercises that will help you ward off negativity before it can get under your skin. But let's look at another common challenge first – when someone else's bad mood begins to drag your mood down.

Let's use an example to demonstrate:

Imagine that you are shopping in a store. You are in a good mood initially, but when you get to the checkout line you notice that the clerk is being rude to everyone. She seems to be angry about something so her whole demeanor is hostile.

Instantly you feel a bit annoyed by her attitude, but you remember that you are trying to focus on the positive so you firmly bite your tongue and say nothing. But with every passing minute she becomes ruder and ruder, until finally you feel ready to scream with frustration.

You manage to check out and leave the store without an altercation, but now your mood has been dampened. Unless you deal with your negative feelings, they will continue to lurk beneath the surface, attracting more and more experiences that annoy you.

If you work through the negative thoughts and feelings first, you will then be able to turn them in a more positive direction. To work through them, you need to process them and then deliberately let them go.

One good way to do this is by talking it out and gradually transitioning from negative to positive as you do so. Let's continue with our rude checkout girl example.

When you get back into your car, you might say something like this:

"Geez, what was her problem? There's no need to be so rude! That annoyed me and now I need to deal with these feelings or they'll stay with me for the rest of the day. Okay, first, I don't know for sure what was happening with that girl. Maybe she's always miserable like that, but maybe not. Maybe her manager just yelled at her minutes before I got there. He might be a real jerk, for all I know. Maybe she just got dumped by her boyfriend last night, or someone she loves passed away recently.

"It's still no excuse for being rude, but I can kind of understand what it's like to be angry or upset and have to deal with demanding customers all day. That can't be easy. In any case, I've decided to let this go. There's no sense hanging onto something so petty. Instead of annoyance, I choose to focus on . . . positive, happy clerks. I remember last week at the hardware store, the guy behind the counter was so helpful! And funny too, he kept me laughing the whole time I was there. I really appreciated that . . ."

Keep going with that line of thought until you have talked yourself into a better place, and within a few minutes you should notice your annoyance dissipating.

This is just an example; you obviously want to let your own thoughts flow naturally – as long as you start from your current place of anger or annoyance (or whatever negative emotion you feel) and then use self-talk to move gradually into a more positive stream of thought.

## Make a Quick Polarity Shift

When you come face to face with a negative attitude, you can also shift to the opposite polarity if you act quickly and firmly enough. A "polarity shift" means quickly and deliberately shifting your focus away from the source of negativity and focusing intently on something more positive.

For example, if one of your coworkers came to you and began complaining bitterly about the company policies and you do not want to be drawn into the negativity, you could excuse yourself to go to the restroom and take a few minutes to focus on something more positive. It can be anything that makes you feel good, like thinking about someone you love, a fond memory or a funny joke you heard recently.

However, this method will only work when you first encounter the negativity. If you don't act quickly enough and wait until you are feeling the effects of negativity, such as anger, depression, frustration or annoyance, you will need to take a more gradual approach, such as using the self-talk method.

When it comes right down to it, you are the only one who can control what you focus on. Encountering negative people does not mean that you have to be negative too. You can choose to stay focused positively, and when you have truly gained control over your thoughts, you will even find it easy to do. In the meantime, the following exercises should help a lot.

## *The Tools: Blocking Negativity Before it Invades Your Focus*

The following tools and techniques can be used as preventative measures to help block negativity before it takes over your mood and mindset, and some of them can also be used in-the-moment when you encounter a negative person.

- **Avoidance**

  Avoiding negativity is not really a "tool" in the official sense, but it's a crucial step that should be taken as often as possible. In some cases it's impossible to avoid negative people because you may work with them, be married to one of them, or be otherwise related to one or more of them.

  However, you may be able to think of at least a few negative people that you frequently spend time with even though you don't really have to. Like an old friend that you once had a lot in common with but don't anymore. Or an associate that you used to work with but no longer do. It's common to hold onto old relationships even if they no longer serve our highest good – and this is especially true for relationships with negative people.

You may be afraid to end the relationship because you think they would hate you or you may feel bad for them because they have such a difficult life (which they endlessly tell you about, over and over and over). But if these types of relationships are causing you a lot of grief, terminating them may be worth the initial discomfort you would experience. If you aren't willing to end these relationships altogether, you can at least make an effort to limit the amount of time you devote to them.

### • Pop Some Negativity Bubbles

Here's a fun way to turn negativity from others into a mental game – almost like a video game that you play in your mind. When you encounter a person who is spewing negativity, imagine that the words coming out of his or her mouth are encased in clear shiny bubbles, and you are holding a big, sharp pin in your hand. Imagine "popping" the negativity bubbles as they zoom toward you, and watch them burst into a shower of glitter or butterflies, or any positive symbol you wish to use.

Obviously, it's a good idea to move away from the negative person eventually because you can't stand there mentally popping bubbles all day, but this method is good for momentary encounters that you can't avoid.

### • No Thank You!

This technique is similar to bubble-popping, but it's even easier because it doesn't require any visualization skills. From this moment on, whenever you encounter a negative person or negativity in any form, you will imagine that they are "offering" their negative energy to you.

Your only job in these situations is to keep mentally saying, "No thank you; no thank you; no thank you; no thank you!" Affirm silently that you don't want their negative energy and you decline to receive it.

Sound too simple to be effective? On the contrary – it works like a charm. In fact, you may even find the whole exercise to be so humorous that you mentally chuckle the whole time, which will further help block negativity.

You can also use this same technique to "decline" negative comments and insults from people. Like if your mother constantly criticizes you; or if your spouse puts down your dreams and goals, you could mentally recite "No thank you" every time they utter one of those negative comments.

This is a great way to reaffirm to yourself that other people's opinions and beliefs do not have to become yours.

### • Step Behind an Iron Shield

If these techniques don't seem strong enough, you can also visualize yourself stepping behind an invisible iron shield that wraps around to your sides, creating a safe, half-circle shape within which you can stand.

See this solid cast iron shield clearly in your mind, and imagine how heavy and immovable it is. Imagine that all negativity coming in your direction smashes against the shield and is deflected away from you.

Once again, this exercise works best if you begin using it before negativity starts to affect you. If you are already annoyed or upset about something, it will probably be less effective.

You can also use this method in a preventative way by spending a few minutes visualizing your iron shield before you start your day, or before you enter into a situation that could turn negative at some point.

### • Stabilize Your Mind and Emotions

Another preventative technique you can use before leaving your home is to spend a few minutes mentally and emotionally "stabilizing" yourself so you feel more balanced. To do this, stand with your feet slightly wider apart than your hips, knees gently bent, as if you were bracing yourself on an unstable surface.

Bring your hands up in front of your chest with both palms touching, like a prayer pose. Close your eyes and take a slow, deep breath in, imagining that you are breathing in empowering energy that spreads quickly from your lungs throughout your entire body. Feel it flowing into your arms, hands, legs and feet, down into the floor beneath you, "anchoring" you in place.

Imagine that this energy also forms a solid core of strength within your torso, from the base of your spine up through the top of your head. Say out loud several times, "I am balanced and centered" and as you say the words, imagine that you can really feel yourself being perfectly balanced and centered in every possible way. Affirm that nothing can knock you off center today; that all negativity will bounce off of you harmlessly.

During the day if you do find yourself feeling unbalanced or overwhelmed, close your eyes and mentally take that pose again and affirm silently, "I am balanced and centered."

## *When Worlds Collide: Creation Conflicts with Spouses and Partners*

The techniques mentioned so far work great with acquaintances, friends, coworkers and other less-influential people in your life, but what can you do about spouses, partners, children and close family members that seem to get in the way of manifesting the life you dream of?

As I mentioned earlier, sometimes we label a person as "negative" when they really aren't. Or at least they don't mean to be. Your spouse may have a few negative things to say if he or she disagrees with your beliefs (like those about the Law of Attraction and conscious creation) or your children may have different ideas about the life they want to live that conflict with your ideas about what's best for them.

In cases like these, they simply have differing perspectives and aspirations than you do. Neither of you are right or wrong – just seeing things differently. Believe it or not, there are endless ways that the universe can satisfy both desires, even if they seem to be contradictory!

When it comes to conflicting desires, the best approach is to focus only on your own dreams and goals, and let the universe handle the rest. Don't worry about whether your spouse would approve or not; don't worry about whether your family would support your decisions – most often these kinds of worries are groundless because your desires will be delivered in a way that is effortless and smooth – and beneficial for everyone concerned, even if you have to work out a few compromises to keep everyone happy.

## Dealing With Genuinely Negative Spouses/Partners

If your spouse's or partner's negativity is not caused by a mere differing opinion or belief, your challenge may be a bit more daunting.

Important Note: With truly destructive or abusive relationships, you may need to make some hard decisions for your own well-being. There are no manifesting techniques that can change an abuser into a kind human being if he or she is not willing to change or seek help.

Beyond severe cases like that, how do you handle a spouse that seems to be so negative that it keeps threatening your positive focus?

First, it may be helpful for you to figure out why he or she is being negative. Here are some questions to get you started:

- Is he/she negative about everything, or just me?

- Why does he/she put down my dreams and goals?

- What are his/her dreams and goals?

- Do they conflict with mine?

- Does he/she believe in Law of Attraction or think it's nonsense?

Once you have an idea about the reasons behind the negativity, you will be in a better position to deal with it effectively.

Some common reasons might be:

- If your partner is a practical person, talk of "manifesting" and the Law of Attraction might seem like pie-in-the-sky nonsense, and your belief in it irritates him/her.

- He or she might fear change, and your goal to improve your life is unnerving.

- He or she might want to believe in conscious creation, but fear looking foolish or naïve.

- Even if his/her negativity is not directed at you, he/she might simply have a chronic habit of negative thinking and speaking, and be unwilling to put forth the effort to change it.

Even if you don't know why he or she is so negative, it doesn't necessarily mean you have to "turn the other cheek" and subject yourself to constant negativity. You can take many different actions, and here are a few that may help:

- **Speak to him or her about your feelings.**

  Example conversation: "I understand that you don't believe in this stuff, but I feel hurt when you put it down because it seems like you're putting me down too. I can respect your beliefs and opinions and I wish you would respect mine too, even if we disagree."

- **Remove yourself from their presence when they start with the negative talk.**

You don't have to make a big issue out of it, just take a trip to the bathroom, the bedroom – or mentally go somewhere else! Part of your mind will still be with your spouse, obviously, but what if another part of you could be calmly strolling along a beautiful ocean beach at sunset? What if you could make it so realistic that you could feel the warm breeze in your hair and the sand between your toes? It may sound silly, but the positive imagery just might be enough to balance out the negativity coming from your spouse.

- **Visualize what you want.**

Just as with ANY desire, visualizing what you want rather than focusing on what you don't want is an excellent way to get energy flowing in the right direction. This goes for your spouse's negativity too.

You may not be able to make him or her be more positive but you can visualize it, can't you? Before you dismiss that idea, try it. Commit to spending 30 days imagining your spouse being the way you want him or her to be. But don't do it to try to make it happen; instead approach it from the mindset of doing it because it makes you feel good. If you like, think back to the time when you first got together. Recall the passion, love and connection you once felt, and relive it mentally and emotionally each day.

At the very least, this exercise will help change your perception of your spouse, which will make you act differently toward him or her, which is likely to change their behavior in positive ways too.

## *All Positive Change Begins With You*

When it comes right down to it, you cannot control what anyone else thinks, says or does. You can't "change" anyone else so that they magically become more positive. But you CAN choose your own thoughts; you can choose your own object of focus; and you can turn away from the things you don't want to perpetuate in your life.

The ideas and techniques we have covered here should give you a great starting place to gain better control over your focus and help you to overcome negativity on a daily basis no matter who it comes from. However, you can devise your own coping techniques too. Simply ask yourself, "I don't want to expand this quality in my life, so what else can I do to make myself feel more positive, joyful, grateful and confident?" Then use those insights as manifesting tools to bring forth the life you desire and deserve.

# Manifesting Under Pressure

## *How to Stay Focused in the Midst of Chaos and Upheaval*

If you are like most deliberate creators, working with the Law of Attraction gives you a strong feeling of excitement and empowerment. When you first conceive a desire, you probably feel optimistic and confident that you can create it easily, and you eagerly begin doing just that. You learn and apply various techniques and methods that can help you to shift your thoughts, boost your vibration and transform your life – and many of them seem to work almost as if by magic.

But then . . . inevitably you bump up against an obstacle. Even if this hasn't yet happened to you, it's far more common than you might think. When this happens to people who are new to using the Law of Attraction, they immediately think they've done something wrong and their manifestation attempts aren't working. More often than not, there are other factors at work – but we'll get to those in a minute.

First, let's explore the types of obstacles you may encounter as you learn to master the Law of Attraction:

You may be working diligently to attract something into your life, meditating and visualizing daily, but it just doesn't seem to be working and days – or even weeks – pass with little progress. Or you may have made some initial progress, but then everything seems to stall for no apparent reason. Or worse, your life circumstances may seem to "blow up" spontaneously, creating chaos and upheaval and preventing you from staying positive and focusing on the things you are trying to manifest.

Has this ever happened to you? If so, you know how frustrating and confusing it can be!

## *An Example of Stressful Chaos*

If you're not yet familiar with this type of upheaval, let's go over an example so you can see it in action. Imagine that you are renting your current home and you have a strong desire to move to a better location. Your lease expires six months from now, so you decide to use the Law of Attraction to manifest a bigger, nicer home before then.

You start out eagerly, fully believing that you can manifest your beautiful new home. You spend time each day visualizing all of the details, feeling excited and optimistic every time you think about it. Not much happens right away, but you don't let that worry you because you still have plenty of time.

Several months later, however, you still haven't made any visible progress, and you're starting to doubt that the Law of Attraction is working. You may start questioning your abilities as a deliberate creator and worrying about what will happen if you don't make progress soon.

And then, everything goes haywire when your landlord tells you that he needs to cancel your lease early and you need to find a new home within 30 days! Can you imagine the stress and pressure you would feel at that moment?

Unfortunately, trying to manifest something good during a high-pressure time like this can seem impossible. How can you possibly stay focused on something positive when disaster may be lurking just around the corner?

There are ways to do it, and we'll be exploring them in this guide. But first let's look at another type of upheaval that can appear unexpectedly.

*Upheaval in Other Areas*

Not only is it possible for chaos to pop up in the area of your life you are trying to improve, but it can also manifest in completely unrelated areas. For example, you may be focused on manifesting a better place to live when you unexpectedly lose your job, your marriage breaks up, your best friend stops speaking to you for no apparent reason, or you develop a serious illness.

When this happens, it may seem as if the universe is playing a cruel joke on you. You may feel shell-shocked, wondering how on earth you could have attracted a nightmare situation like this when you were so diligent about staying focused on something good!

Questions like these may keep swirling through your mind: "Why is this happening to me? What am I doing wrong? Why isn't the Law of Attraction working for me?"

**The True Causes of Upheaval**

There are many possible causes for upheavals like these and it's not because the universe is picking on you or playing a cruel joke. There is usually a deeper process being played out.

Here are a few of the most common causes:

- **Your desire is still too new.**

If you have just begun working with the Law of Attraction, you may still be receiving "residual" manifestations that were created by previous negative thought patterns. As you begin transforming your thoughts and beliefs, little by little your outer circumstances should begin to reflect that positive focus, but it does take time.

- **The universe is making room for your new circumstances.**

Another possibility is that situations that no longer serve you are being cleared away to make room for much better circumstances. But when the new, better circumstances haven't quite shown up yet, it can leave you feeling unbalanced and frightened – and wondering what on earth is causing all this "destruction."

- **You may be sabotaging your own desires.**

Subconsciously it's possible for you to attract difficult circumstances to distract yourself and sabotage your efforts to manifest something good. Why would you do this? If the outcome you are trying to attract scares you or intimidates you in any way, your natural inclination will be to avoid it at all costs.

Without even realizing it, you may attract chaotic and difficult circumstances so that you will have an excuse not to work on attracting something better – or you may attract events and circumstances that directly prevent you from creating your desired outcome.

- **You may be trying to force something to happen (trying too hard).**

When it comes to manifestation, trying to force something to happen quickly is one of the worst things you can do because it only causes more delays. When you try too hard, you usually have an inner sense of "urgency," which communicates to the universe that you would like more situations that make you feel pressured and urgent. Obviously, you won't be able to attract situations that make you feel calm and satisfied either.

- **You may be trying to control "how" the outcome happens.**

Just as detrimental as trying to hurry a manifestation along is trying to control how everything unfolds. This usually happens when you become emotionally attached to a specific "way" that you want the outcome to be delivered – which is usually the result of not trusting that the universe can easily find the fastest and best way to deliver your desires.

When you do this, you end up blocking other possibilities, which creates more delays.

**The Worse it Gets, the Worse it Gets!**

The more stressed and pressured you feel, and the more you try to "hurry up and manifest" your desired outcome, the longer it's going to take. And the more you focus on your feelings of frustration and panic, the more resistance you will throw into the mix, which just creates more blockages and delays.

You may be wondering if it's even possible to NOT feel pressured in these kinds of situations. Isn't it natural to feel anxious and urgent? Yes. But there are simple ways to release those feelings and stay focused on what you want, and we're going to explore several of them in this guide.

**Everyday Stress Can Interfere With Successful Manifesting Too**

Even if you aren't dealing with major upheavals, you may have a lot of daily stressors that keep you feeling frustrated and tense. Perhaps your job is very stressful, or some of your relationships seem to be in a negative place, or you otherwise feel "on edge" much of the time.

Feeling this way can often hold back the things you are trying to attract, simply because you are not in alignment with the essence of them.

It's hard to allow in financial abundance when you're focusing on how tired and stressed you feel. It's hard to allow in vibrant health when you're focusing on a shortage of love and intimacy in your relationships. No matter what you are trying to attract, you need to be consistently aligned energetically with the essence of it – and all of the situations in your life are interconnected. Imbalance or disharmony in one area can affect all of the others.

## *How to Manifest Under Pressure*

The title of this guide refers to "manifesting under pressure" – but that phrase is really an oxymoron. It's not possible to "manifest under pressure." By that, I mean that experiencing feelings of pressure, stress, anxiety, sadness, or any other "negative" quality can ONLY attract more situations in which you feel badly.

To manifest something positive, you need to release the negative feelings that would block it and move into a more positive state of mind and emotion, which will allow the better circumstances to manifest. That doesn't mean that you have to resolve all of the upheavals in your life before you will make progress with your manifestations. It does mean that you have to find a way to feel better, even if you haven't yet received the better conditions you want.

The definition of "stress" as most of us perceive it, is a feeling of tension or pressure caused by internal or external factors. However, it is our own thoughts that trigger this feeling of tension or pressure. A good way to look at this is to consider why certain people thrive on high-pressured situations, while others feel overwhelmed by them. For example, the thought of skydiving out of an airplane may excite you, while it may terrify me. You may tremble at the thought of speaking in front of a group of people, while I might be eager to do so.

Each of us feels scared, stressed or overwhelmed by different experiences. And those feelings of stress and pressure get started according to what we're THINKING at the time. Using the public speaking example again, if you felt stressed by the idea of speaking to a large group of people, your inner chatter would be saying things like, "No way! I can't get up and speak in front of those people; I'll just make a fool of myself! I can't do it; I'm just not good at that kind of thing!" And the more you think thoughts like that, the more stressed you are going to feel.

If I enjoyed public speaking, my thoughts would be more like this, "Good, I can do this! I've got some great ideas I'd like to share with the group; they're going to love these. This will be fun!"

Depending on the direction of your thoughts, your feelings will follow suit.

**Identify the Sources of Your Stress**

The important question to ask yourself is, "What causes the most stress in my life?" If you are currently dealing with big upheavals and chaos like we covered earlier, then you already know. But if it's just everyday stress that is keeping you blocked, you may have to make a list of the situations and experiences that commonly make you feel pressured.

Then your job is to consider whether any of those situations could be effectively removed from your life (like destructive relationships), or, if they cannot be removed (like health challenges), changing your thoughts about them to ease your feelings of tension.

With every situation in your life, the goal is the same: to feel **at peace about it.**

You may be thinking that you can't possibly feel at peace about some of your current challenges, but it's not as difficult as it seems. Feeling at peace about something doesn't mean you have to give up on manifesting something better; it just means not fighting against what is already here in your life. The best part is, once you feel at peace about a situation, you dissolve any blockages your feelings of dissatisfaction were causing, and you allow the better situation you want to come through easily!

**How to Move into a Peaceful State of Mind**

There are many different ways to deal with feelings of stress and pressure, but there are a key few that seem to work extremely well with the Law of Attraction too:

- **Meditation & Visualization**

  Meditation is like a miracle tool that can instantly dissolve resistance in your energetic signal. And the best part is that it's so simple that anyone can do it. The easiest meditation method is to sit calmly, breathe slowly and deeply, and do your best to quiet your mind. Ten or fifteen minutes of this daily can do wonders for your stress level! With consistent effort, you will notice that your manifestations start moving along much more smoothly and quickly because you are giving your mind a break from its habitual focus on negativity.

Visualization also works well, but it can take a bit more practice to master it. Simply call to mind something that makes you feel peaceful or happy. If you like, you can visualize the very situation(s) that are causing you stress, and imagine that they are more harmonious. For example, if you feel panicky about having to find a new home quickly, close your eyes and spend 10 minutes imagining that you have already found the perfect residence and you no longer need to panic.

Allow feelings of relief and peacefulness to flow through your mind and body. Or, you can visualize something unrelated that also makes you feel at peace – generating the peaceful feeling is what is most important, no matter how you get there.

## • Write Out the Perfect Solution

A fun way to quickly move into a more peaceful, happy state of mind is to write out a perfect solution to the situations that are making you feel stressed.

Start by thinking about the situation, and then write in a notebook or journal, "I can imagine what it would be like if this problem was resolved. If I had just found the perfect new home and I was going to sign the lease tomorrow, I would feel so excited!" Keep going by writing down all of the details exactly as you wish them to be.

And as you write, allow those happy feelings to flow through you and make the experience as real as possible. By the time you finish writing, you should notice that you feel much less pressured.

## • Create a Relaxation Trigger

This method is extremely helpful when you are in the midst of a stressful situation and cannot take time to meditate, write or use more focused techniques. However, it does require some effort before it will be completely effective.

Every day, spend a few minutes performing a specific physical trigger while also saying a few words (or a mantra) that help you to relax. For example, you can pinch your thumb and pinky finger together and say, "All is well, all is well, all is well." Or tap your chin lightly and say, "I am completely at peace right now."

The actions and words don't matter except that you do them the same way each time. As you say the words, really feel a sensation of peace and well-being flowing through you. When you do this every day, you begin to connect the action and words with a sense of well-being.

When you find yourself in a stressful situation, you can "trigger" yourself into a state of peace and well-being by making the motion and mentally reciting the words again.

### • Staying Calm and Detached

Now that you know that your own thoughts are the cause of your stress, you can begin taking greater control over them when you find yourself in a stressful situation. One good way to do this is by setting a daily intention to stay calm and detached no matter what happens.

The moment you start to feel stressed, recognize it and say to yourself, "All right, I'm starting to feel stressed, so it's time to take a deep breath and step back emotionally from this situation." Focus on relaxing your body, letting go of stressful thoughts, and seeing the situation objectively.

This definitely takes time to master, but practice makes perfect.

### • Choosing Better Beliefs

Your thoughts are a powerful trigger for stressful feelings, but when you add in strong beliefs to the mix, it can intensify the situation even more. Going back to our housing example, in the moment when you discover that you have to move within 30 days your thoughts will probably swing in a negative direction: "Great, this is just what I needed – now what am I going to do?"

But if you also have limiting or negative beliefs that are activated by the situation, your perception will be altered even more by them and your thoughts might continue into something more negative, like this: "I should have known; things like this always happen to me. Now I'll have to scramble to find a crappy little apartment that's even worse than the one I had. This Law of Attraction stuff doesn't work; I knew it all along."

The limiting belief that nothing ever works out for you is now making you feel even more stressed because you believe it means that you will end up living in worse conditions rather than better ones.

But is this necessarily true? No – it's a perception! And in that moment, when the negative belief pops up, you have the power to choose something better.

You might say something like this: "Wow, where did those thoughts come from? Just because things don't appear to be working out like I planned doesn't mean they still can't work out. In fact, maybe this is all happening for a good reason. Maybe there is a gorgeous apartment that is ready for me right now and I would have missed it if I stayed here another month or two!"

You can even take it further by deliberately choosing a great outcome, despite how things may appear right now. "I intend that something really great comes from this situation. I intend that the universe is working on my behalf and I will be led to the perfect solution – something even better than I could have orchestrated on my own!"

Never underestimate the power of belief! The more convinced you are that all is well, the more quickly and easily circumstances can shift to make it so.

## *Examples: How to Use These Techniques*

Some of the most common manifestations that people try to achieve are related to money, health and relationships – but these are also some of the most emotionally charged situations in our lives, and therefore they can be the most challenging to transform.

Let's go over some examples of stressful situations so you can see how to use the techniques we've explored to ease the pressure and still manifest wonderful outcomes.

## *Financial Challenges*

Undoubtedly, financial challenges are some of the most stressful situations we can face in life. Especially when we have more expenses than income, or when we keep trying desperately to improve our lives but are consistently held back by financial obstacles. These types of challenges can create a sense of deep despair that detracts from our enjoyment of life in all other areas. Finding ways to stay calm in this type of situation is vital because you cannot allow abundance into your life when you are overwhelmed with stress and anxiety. But how can you stay calm when you may be facing financial disaster?

Most of the techniques we've covered so far would probably be helpful, but especially "Writing Out the Perfect Solution." The biggest challenge with financial problems is that you can't seem to help but obsess over them. All day long you have a chattering voice in the back of your mind saying: "I don't know what to do about these financial problems. I need to get more money coming in. Here's another bill I can't pay; when will it stop? I have to do something but I don't know what to do! I can't stand this pressure anymore!" And the more you focus on thoughts like these, the more stressed you feel, which attracts more stressful situations, which makes you feel even more stressed, and it just keeps going like that.

But writing out the perfect solution is a great way to interrupt the negative cycle and begin focusing on better thoughts, which will trigger better feelings, which will alter the signal you are emitting to the universe, which will begin attracting more abundance into your life.

Here's an example of writing out the perfect financial solution:

"I can imagine how great it would be to allow more money to flow easily into my life. It would be incredible if I was offered a much higher-paying job, something that I truly enjoyed doing. I love the idea of waking up in the morning, excited to get to work because I have so much fun doing it. And of course, I would love receiving those big paychecks each week too! The first thing I would do is pay off all of my bills so I was debt free. Then I would buy a nicer car, and maybe even buy the house I've always wanted. I would be able to help my family by giving them some money, and I would also love to help out some worthy causes financially too."

Keep going for as long as you like, focusing on scenarios that make you feel really good. Doing this on a regular basis (daily, if possible) is an excellent way to begin shifting your thoughts about money from negative to positive.

## Relationship Challenges

Relationship problems are another common cause of stress because you automatically feel like you have to focus on the negative aspects in order to change them – but that won't work with the Law of Attraction! Two good examples of relationship challenges:

1) If you are currently involved in a relationship that has become dissatisfying or problematic, you probably spend more time focusing on the qualities in your partner (or boss, friend, coworker) that you do not like or appreciate. And the more you focus on those negative traits, the more difficult it will be to manifest the healthy relationship you want.

2) If you are desperately trying to attract a romantic partner, you may have a difficult time believing that there is someone out there for you, which makes you feel anxious that you may be alone forever. Or you may believe that he or she will eventually show up but it seems to be taking a very long time. You may feel pressured that time is running out – or you may simply feel lonely and have a hard time tuning into the essence of being in a loving relationship.

Both of these examples have the same thing in common: you are focusing more on what you don't want rather than what you do want. Turning this trend around is as simple as changing the way you see your current reality. Rather than continuing the perception of a flawed relationship (or no relationship), you can use one or more of the techniques we covered earlier in this guide.

For example:

**Staying calm and detached**

When conflict arises in your current relationship(s), do you often react with anger, frustration or emotional turmoil? When you think about the loving relationship you deeply desire but don't yet have, does it make you feel emotionally empty? These feelings will only keep attracting more of the same type of situations, so it's a good idea to get control of them – and staying calm and detached is a good way to start.

The next time you feel your emotions beginning to move into a negative place regarding a relationship issue, pause for a moment and take a deep breath. Say to yourself, "I'm stepping back from this situation emotionally because getting upset won't solve anything. I choose to feel peaceful and clear-headed regarding this situation. I want to attract something better and I need to adjust my thinking to do it." Then focus on what you WANT to happen in this situation.

That doesn't mean your desire will form immediately. (In fact, it probably won't.) But the more you do this, the calmer you'll start to feel on a regular basis – and that will have an impact on your ability to allow in the healthier relationships you desire.

## *Health Challenges*

Health challenges can also cause excessive stress, which makes it impossible to manifest a better health condition – and a vicious circle is once again formed, keeping you trapped in the current reality. Meditation and visualization are extremely effective when it comes to health conditions, because it has been proven repeatedly that healing can happen more quickly and easily when you feel relaxed and happy. Stress only exacerbates illness and poor health conditions.

Here's a great example of a meditation/visualization that you can use to focus on better health and well-being: Set aside 20 to 30 minutes for yourself and find a quiet place where you can lie down in a comfortable position. Close your eyes and begin relaxing your body, breathing slowly and deeply, and releasing stressful thoughts.

When you feel completely relaxed, engage in some positive self-talk, either out loud or silently: "I am willing to be completely well again. My body is now moving back into a state of perfect well-being. I am eager to feel strong and vibrant again. I give myself permission to be well . . ."

As you say or think the words, see yourself in your mind's eye, being completely healthy and strong and feeling amazing! Tune in to these feelings as best you can and stay with them for five to 10 minutes, or longer if you like.

When you are done visualizing, you can either get up and continue on with your day, or spend a few more moments affirming perfect health and well-being.

When you do continue with your normal activities, pay attention to the way your body feels. If you start to notice that pain, discomfort, nausea or your usual symptoms are beginning to return, it may be an indication that your energy is starting to slip out of alignment with wellness again.

Ideally that would be a great time to sit or lie down and repeat the meditation/visualization again; if you can't, at least try to do it again later when you have the time and opportunity.

**Letting Go of Negativity is Your Sole Objective**

The techniques in these examples don't necessarily have to be used only for those situations – mix and match them however you like. Or, if you already have a favorite method to calm stress and feel good, by all means use it as often as possible.

The whole point is to let go of negativity and limiting thoughts so that you can allow your desired outcome(s) to manifest more quickly.

Remember that your reaction to stress and chaos plays a big part in the final outcome. If you panic and get upset, circumstances from that moment on will become more turbulent. If you remain calm, confident and optimistic, no matter how bleak things may appear at first glance, you will contribute that calm, peaceful energy to the outcome.

Finally, always keep in mind that the upheavals and stress are momentary – they will pass, and when they do, you will begin moving forward again much more quickly and easily than you did before.

# Detached Manifesting

*How to Let Go, Trust, and Believe that Your Desires Are on the Way!*

Undoubtedly, one of the most vital parts of the manifestation process is the process of letting go and trusting that your desires are being delivered by the universe. Unfortunately, this is also one of the things that people struggle with most often. Do you?

Let's face it; it's easy to decide that you want something, imagine how great it will be to have it, create vision boards and written descriptions, and recite affirmations about it – but it's not so easy to believe it's coming if you haven't yet had a lot of experience in manifesting successfully.

This guide is going to show you just how easy it can be to create a solid habit of letting go, trusting, and truly believing that the universe is working on your behalf.

If you aren't yet aware of just how powerful your beliefs are when it comes to manifestation, let's just say that your beliefs form the "filter" of what you will allow (or disallow) into your life. Whatever you believe is what you will receive.

## *Beliefs That Can Hold Back Your Manifestations*

There are endless beliefs that have the power to block your desires, but there are several that seem to be most common:

### 1) "The universe doesn't care about me."

Do you hold a perception of the universe as being distant, unfeeling, or even judgmental? Perhaps you were raised to believe that "God" was cruel and vengeful, or perhaps you once asked the universe for help with something and didn't receive it so you concluded that your request wasn't heard, was outright denied, or that you were "meant" to suffer.

Regardless of why you may feel that way, this kind of belief can absolutely hold back your desires because you will keep communicating to the universe, "I want this thing but I know you won't let me have it." And the universe simply conforms to your belief.

### 2) "I don't deserve it."

Perhaps on an intellectual level you know that you deserve to have the things you want, but deep down inside on an emotional level do you really believe it? Many people don't – and they are shocked when they recognize this belief within themselves.

Believe it or not, it's possible to consider yourself a pretty positive person, a basically good person, and still have an underlying belief that you're somehow not good enough, not talented enough, not "whatever" enough to deserve the things you want.

### 3) "I'm not sure I can manifest that."

Many people who are fairly new to deliberate creation still don't have a solid belief in their own abilities, and this can result in shaky intentions and sporadic results. Over time your belief will grow naturally as you gain knowledge and confidence, but in the meantime you may struggle with feelings of inadequacy and uncertainty.

### 4) "If I let go, it won't happen."

The fear of not receiving what you want is a powerful motivator that can keep you "clinging" to your intentions and refusing to allow the universe to work on your behalf. Again, this may stem from a belief that the universe is unkind or distant, or your lack of belief in your own ability to work in partnership with the universe, or any number of other causes.

Unfortunately, the message you will keep communicating with this belief is one of doubt and resistance, which cannot manifest anything good.

### 5) "I have to do it all myself if I want it done right."

This belief is usually the result of a perfectionism mind-set, and if you struggle with this it will likely show up in other areas of your life too. Most often it stems from a fear that you won't get the outcome you want unless you do it yourself – which unfortunately becomes a self-fulfilling prophecy! Distrust can be a strong contributor to this belief too.

## *How to Change Limiting Beliefs into Positive Beliefs*

These common limiting beliefs and others have been formed over many days, months and years of consistent reinforcement throughout your lifetime. As the beliefs were formed and strengthened, and as you expected to experience things related to these beliefs, you actually manifested them.

That may be hard to believe, but think back for a moment; can you remember any experiences where you believed something unpleasant would happen and it did? Have you ever expected something awful to happen and it did?

Likewise, you can probably remember at least a few times where you expected or believed something good would happen and it did. It works both ways, and these experiences demonstrate one thing: beliefs are powerful!

How can you change such deeply ingrained beliefs that you may have been reinforcing for years and years? You may be surprised at just how easily it can be done!

Here are three good ways to start:

- **Analyze them logically**

  Some beliefs made sense to us when we were children, but seem ludicrous when we think about them now. For example, believing that you're not good enough, or believing that it's greedy to want to be financially successful.

  For every one of your limiting beliefs, write it down

and spend some time really thinking about it. Is it really true that you're not good enough? Can you come up with one good reason why you don't deserve to have the things you want? Can you come up with a list of at least 10 reasons why you DO?

The more you question limiting beliefs like this, the more you realize just how funny some of them can be – and how quickly you can change them once you realize they are untrue.

### • Repetition, Repetition, Repetition

The way your existing beliefs were so deeply ingrained into your consciousness is through the use of repetition. The more you told yourself that something was true, the more deeply you believed it.

The good news is that you can use this very same process to install positive beliefs. Simply make a list of positive beliefs you would like to have, such as:

"I am good enough. I am a great person. I deserve to be happy. I deserve to be abundant. The universe loves me. The universe is always looking out for me and working on my behalf." And begin speaking or writing them down every single day, many times a day.

This doesn't have to be quite as labor-intensive as it sounds; simply create an ongoing self-talk routine where you mentally state these positive beliefs all day long while you're doing other things.

The more you say them, and the more you write them down, the more firmly entrenched in your mind they are going to become.

- **Look for evidence**

Another important reason why some of your beliefs may seem unshakable is because you have received "evidence" to support them.

For example, if you didn't feel loved as a child, you may have concluded that you were unlovable. Emotionally distant or even abusive parents or caregivers could have convinced you that there was something wrong with you, and that you didn't deserve to be loved.

As an adult you can decide that that's not true, but to your child's mind the "evidence" seemed to be clear and incriminating – your parents or caregivers not expressing their love to you.

However, you can also proactively build your positive beliefs by looking for "evidence" that they are true. Very few of us have had all "bad" experiences in life; there are also a fair number of positive experiences from which we can gather some empowering evidence.

Example: Have you ever had the experience where you struggled and struggled with a problem for a long time, and finally said to the universe (or God), "That's it; I give up; I cannot handle this anymore, so I'm turning it over to you." And almost as if by magic, a solution came along shortly thereafter?

Or, have you ever asked for guidance on something and had the answer show up in the most surprising, wonderful way?

Experiences like these can provide the evidence you need to develop an unshakable belief in a loving, kind, benevolent universe that is eager to give you everything you want.

## *Letting Go of "How" It All Comes Together*

Even after you have built up your belief that you deserve the things you want, that the universe loves you and wants you to be happy, and that your requests are being heard and processed – you may still struggle to truly believe that the universe can find the best possible way to deliver your desires.

This is one of the biggest challenges that deliberate creators face because we simply can't see the "big picture" like the universe can. Instead we get attached to a specific scenario that we THINK is the best way to have our desire satisfied, and we refuse to allow any other possibilities!

Have you ever done this?

Here are some great, easy ideas to help you let go of the "how" and truly trust that the universe has it all under control.

## 1) Focus on the ESSENCE of your desire.

The first step is to get clear about what you really want – NOT what you think you can get based on what you believe is possible. There is a big difference between the two.

Many people say, "I really want this outcome but I doubt it will happen, so I will settle for this other outcome instead." The second outcome really isn't what they want, so they either end up with an outcome that doesn't satisfy them, or they simply can't generate enough energy toward the outcome so nothing changes at all.

Here's a vital secret that will create miracles in your life if you embrace it: everything you want has an ESSENCE – or a FEELING – behind it. When you desire a bigger income, you don't really care about the money itself; you care about how having that money will make you feel. You want those feelings of inner peace, security, joy, freedom, and so on.

When you set an intention or goal, your job as a deliberate creator is to get clear on what you want and WHY you want it. In other words, the essence of what you're really after.

It's okay to imagine specific situations if they generate the feelings you desire. For example, imagining that you have a lot of money can absolutely attune you to the essence of abundance. But what you don't want to do is get hooked on only one way that abundance can come to you. (We'll go into this further in a moment.)

## 2) Express your desire clearly to the universe.

You really don't have to do this step in any kind of formal way, because the moment you conceive a desire the universe "gets the message." But officially asking for something can help you feel as if you are proactively communicating your request, which can also help build your belief that the universe heard you and is already working on it.

To express your desire officially, you can state it out loud: "I intend to manifest an income of $50,000 a year."

You can also write it down in the same format; or write it more like a journal entry that is happening in real time. Example: "I am now earning a salary of $50,000 a year doing work I absolutely love, and I'm so happy about that!"

Go on to include plenty of details about the scenario as you wish it to play out, and have fun with it.

You really only have to express your intention once, but you can also work on it every day if you like. The benefit to doing this is that it will help keep your thoughts focused on what you want, rather than complaining about the way things are now.

### 3) Surrender the entire goal to the universe.

Even if you continue to spend time focusing on your desire each day, you also need to detach and LET GO of it at the same time. That doesn't mean you can't think about it at all; it simply means you cannot be emotionally attached to when and how it will arrive.

Part of this process requires that you believe and trust that the universe heard your request and is working on it. Another part requires a belief that you deserve to have it, and you will have it. If you still have trouble with these beliefs, keep working on them daily and gradually you will build them up.

Here's how to tell if you are attached or detached:

**Attached** – You will find yourself obsessing about your goal, constantly wondering and worrying about when it's coming and how it might work out. You may even feel an urge to take drastic action to "make it happen" quickly. Any and all of these activities are incredibly destructive to the manifestation process and will only cause delays.

**Detached** – You will feel calm, at peace, confident in the certainty that your desire will manifest at the perfect time, and in the perfect way. You will feel content with your present circumstances, even if they aren't what you would prefer to have – you will simply make the best of them and do what you can to feel happy anyway.

Obviously, you are striving to be a detached as possible!

## 4) Use Proactive Belief to convince yourself that it's on the way.

"Proactive belief" can be incredibly helpful when you keep slipping back into a state of attachment.

For the first several days after you set an intention, keep repeating something like this to yourself: "I don't know how or when, but the universe is going to put this all together for me in the most amazing way! I have no way of proving it, but I choose to believe it anyway. I know in my heart that it will all work out wonderfully."

Even if you don't really believe what you're saying, say it anyway! Keep insisting that you believe it, and your belief will steadily grow. And as your belief steadily grows, you'll start to notice shifts taking place in your outer surroundings. This shift will provide a bit of "evidence" that things are indeed progressing.

Proactive belief is also a great way to overcome feelings of doubt about your own ability to manifest what you want. Doubt and uncertainty are easy to recognize; they trigger a twinge of discomfort and anxiety when you think about your intentions.

If you experience this, simply go through the same proactive belief process and INSIST that you believe it is all working out, that you will master this deliberate creation process, and that the universe is behind you all the way.

It may take time to fully believe it, but eventually your belief will be so strong that there will be no denying it.

**5) Don't jump the gun with massive action . . . yet.**

Now, here is where many deliberate creators interfere with the manifestation process. There is a school of thought out there that says action is always necessary to manifest what you want; that you must set your intention and then immediately take massive action to bring the desired outcome into physical form.

This isn't such a bad way to approach life because there is a lot to be said for good old-fashioned "elbow grease" – but this action also demonstrates a great lack of trust in the universe!

By taking immediate action, you are in effect communicating to the universe that you can't (or won't) wait for guidance; you're going to just run out there and make it all happen on your own. In which case, the universe usually says, "Okay, go right ahead."

There's nothing wrong with doing it all on your own – but then that's not "manifesting" change, it's creating change through physical action. Big difference!

A much better approach is to first set your intention, spend time visualizing and affirming that it's yours, build up your belief, and then be on the lookout for an INSPIRED action. "Inspired" in this case means that the universe will let you know if there is anything you need to do to help the process along.

An inspired action will always, always, always feel really good and be relatively easy. That's very different than taking massive action in an effort to make something happen. When you try to make something happen and work really hard on it, all you do is wear yourself out and make very little progress.

On the other hand, inspired actions seem to flow along like water. You get an idea to do something, and even if you're not sure if it will pan out, you still feel excited about it and do it easily – and more often than not, amazing things will come from that one action.

However, note that the results may not be instant. Sometimes it may take a day or a week – but then it's like a floodgate opened and all kinds of amazing progress takes place just because you did that one little thing.

One final caution: if you currently hold a belief that you MUST take action to get the process underway, then it's likely that not much will happen unless you take action.

> To remedy this, you can either work on transforming your belief so that you feel as if the universe is taking care of it, or you can simply come up with a few modest action steps you can take, while also staying on the lookout for inspired actions.
>
> Ideally, it's best to wait for inspired actions because through those insights and hunches the universe is going to show you the fastest, easiest, and most beneficial path to the outcome you desire. You can probably find dozens or hundreds of other ways too, but they won't be as easy or quick.

You may be surprised to know that in many cases, setting an intention to receive something is all you need to do – and the universe will simply deliver it right to you if you are patient enough and truly believe it's coming.

The more proficient you become at manifestation, the more you will probably see this happening. If you are still new to it, however, it may take a bit of work to build up your belief and patience to that level.

You should also become better at discerning when you are being given an inspired action.

*How to Tell When You Are Being Given an Inspired Action*

Some people get confused by this process because they haven't yet fully developed their intuition. They'll get an idea about something and wonder, "Is this an inspired action, or just wishful thinking?"

You will come to realize fairly quickly that inspired actions usually feel like a very strong URGE to do something specific. If you try to ignore the urge, it will get stronger and stronger. Something within you (your intuition) will be poking and prodding at you, practically yelling, "HEY, I'm trying to get your attention!!!"

Even better, the action that you are being prodded to take will always be something fun, easy or enjoyable in some way. If it creates a feeling of fear or resistance within you, it's probably not an inspired action.

However, note that it is possible to feel uncertain or a little nervous about taking an inspired action, but this is different than feeling downright fearful. The slight feelings of uncertainty and nervousness are usually caused by doubt about whether you're really receiving an inspired action, or whether the action will yield any good results or not.

In this case, you might think about the possible negative repercussions of taking the action. Could anything negative come from it? More often than not, the answer will be no, in which case you'll decide to take the action and see what happens.

Even if you decide not to take the action at this time, that's okay! The universe will never force you to do something you don't want to do. It will simply offer suggestions, create opportunities and provide the guidance you ask for – but you have the option to take it or leave it.

And if you don't get that feeling that you're being prodded to do something? Simply keep affirming that the universe is taking care of everything and you'll know when it's time to take action yourself.

## *Letting Go During Times of Crisis*

All of the concepts we have covered so far work great when you're trying to manifest something simple or fun. But what about when you are stuck in really negative circumstances and desperately need to get out of them? What if time is of the essence and you need to make progress FAST?

During times like this it can seem monumentally difficult to let go and trust. In fact, most people go the complete opposite way with their thoughts and slip into a state of panic, fear and urgency that only makes their circumstances worse.

Here are some helpful tips on letting go and trusting during a crisis:

**1) Be willing to accept the worst-case scenario.**

This is probably the most difficult thing to do, so I am listing it first – the rest of the techniques get easier from here.

Being willing to accept the worst-case scenario is probably the last thing you want to do, or anyone wants to do – and yet, that very willingness holds great power!

When you fear something awful happening, you are infusing the possibility with a lot of energy. And as you know, directing your energy and focus toward something – especially something you don't want – is not a good idea! The harder you try to resist it, the stronger it seems to get.

When you stop resisting and instead accept that the worst could possibly happen and if it did you would still be okay, you suddenly experience a rush of freedom and peacefulness. You realize that even though something unpleasant could be lurking around the corner, you're still okay in this moment.

**2) Surrender.**

We've already covered "letting go" in other sections, and surrender is similar. But in a crisis situation, surrender takes on a deeper meaning. Surrender means completely letting go of trying to make a certain outcome happen in the way or timeframe that you want it to. It means turning the entire situation over to the universe and trusting that the best possible outcome will transpire.

Once again, this requires a steady belief that the universe is working with you, cares about you and wants you to be happy. If you don't yet have that strong belief, surrender may feel terrifying at first – but once you relax and open your mind and heart to whatever comes, you will experience an amazing sense of lightness and inner peace that is hard to describe.

### 3) Trust and expect the best.

Many times during a crisis, we automatically expect the worst to happen. Even if there are a million possible ways that things could turn out, we jump right to the worst of them and obsess over the fact that we don't want it to happen.

But it is during times of crisis that we NEED to exercise our power as deliberate creators! And in fact, it is during these times that your power is strongest because you have a passionate desire for a beneficial outcome. If you apply that burning desire to an intention and allow it to fuel your belief, you'll be astounded at how easily you can turn things around!

Simply think about the crisis situation and ask yourself what you would like to have happen – not what you fear happening or what you think could happen. Then gather your inner determination and choose it. Tell the universe firmly that you want "this outcome" to happen (state the actual outcome), and know in your heart that it will.

You may still feel twinges of doubt, and that's all right. When the doubts come, simply reaffirm your faith and insist that the best possible outcome will be yours. Trust, let go and expect positive things to happen – and quite frequently that's exactly what will happen.

## Learn to See Crises As Great Opportunities!

None of us likes going through crises. They are painful, terrifying, unsettling, inconvenient and humbling. But in the context of deliberate creation, they provide opportunities that are unlike any we will receive in other life experiences.

Rather than resisting or cowering in fear during a crisis situation, grasp it as an opportunity to exercise your right to choose what you wish to experience. Say to yourself, "All right, this is not good, but I can choose what happens from here. I choose _____ and I expect this outcome to be mine." Then keep working on building your belief, strengthening your trust, and working in partnership with the universe. The more you do this, and the more you deliberately exercise your inner power in this way, the stronger and more empowered you will feel.

## Detached Manifesting = Letting Go of Resistance

All of the techniques we have covered in this guide have a common goal: they help you to release resistance and dissolve blockages so that your desired outcome(s) can more easily manifest.

That doesn't mean they will every single time, and it doesn't mean that everything will happen instantly – but the odds of successful manifesting are certainly much higher than they will be if you struggle and fight the whole way.

The more you practice being detached, and the more you work on building a solid level of belief in yourself and the universe, the faster and more frequently you will see astounding results from your efforts.

# SECTION II

# 17 WAYS TO ATTRACT ABUNDANCE

The Law of Attraction has become a hot mainstream topic over the past several years, and now more than ever people are realizing that they have control over their physical environment through the use of deliberate thought, positive emotion and conscious intention.

As empowering and thrilling as this new awakening is, the information itself is not new. For centuries spiritual teachers and authors have been sharing profound insights about the power we have to mold and shape our physical surroundings, but this information was not widely available to the majority of "average" people like it is today. Thanks to the Internet and greater availability of books and other media for nearly everyone, we can share information much more quickly and easily than in years past.

Even better, scientific advances over the past century are beginning to provide tentative proof that these concepts work. Quantum exploration is revealing some startling insights into the way our universe operates and we are becoming keenly aware that we are NOT just passive observers but rather powerful participants in our reality, both collective and individual – with the power to exert our will upon our environment and alter the course of our lives.

These studies are helping us to understand exactly how to use the Law of Attraction purposefully to create better, richer, more fulfilling lives. More than ever before, we understand that our actions, thoughts and emotional states will help us to emit the right "frequency" to attract specific experiences into our lives.

The majority of this section focuses on money and

abundance, but the concepts could just as easily be applied to any other subject too. When it comes right down to it, "abundance" is simply our natural state of well-being that includes a constant flow of money, happiness, love, peace, vibrant health and all forms of goodness.

In the following pages you will discover 17 simple things you can do to begin attracting greater abundance into your life. They are presented in no particular order, so read them in any fashion you desire. You can skip around or read the whole book straight through – it's up to you.

Some of these techniques may not be new to you, but consider them seriously anyway. If they are included in this section, it's for one simple reason: they WORK!

One of the most important insights you will gain from this book is that attracting greater abundance into your life isn't only about what you DO but who you ARE; the way you think and feel and believe in every moment of every day. Of course, physical action has its place too, and we'll be discussing that later in the book.

In the meantime, most of the strategies in this book will show you how to shift effortlessly into the mental and emotional state of a person who NATURALLY attracts abundance. In fact, you'll probably experience what many people who practice these techniques do; money flowing into your life from endless sources – both expected and unexpected! Even better, you won't have to struggle and strain to make it happen. It will be a natural by-product of improving the quality of your mental and emotional "frequency."

The length of time it takes to see results will vary greatly from person to person. It all depends on your current "default frequency" and how completely you are able to move into a higher frequency. It is very possible to see results immediately when using these techniques, but even if it takes a bit longer, do not make the mistake of thinking that they aren't working! Some people may experience an apparent lull for a few days to a few weeks – and then BOOM! – everything changes in a heartbeat.

Whether it takes a few minutes or a few months to see results, remember that the more focus you can give these techniques on a daily basis, the more powerful your results will be. Having fun with the whole process will also go a long way in creating rapid results.

All right, are you ready to begin attracting abundance? Let's go!

## #1 – *Switch Your Focus*

One of the most important (and usually most challenging) things you can do to attract abundance is get into the habit of purposely switching your focus away from lack and scarcity. This can be difficult to do because most people who are heavily focused on lack don't even know it!

What do I mean by "focused" on lack? I mean thinking about it almost constantly. Worrying about how the bills will be paid. Worrying about whether there will be "enough" money for the things you need. Noticing with envy and bitterness how others seem to have so much more than you do. Agonizing and railing against the fact that you have so little.

Feeling fearful, insecure and frustrated about financial issues . . . and it goes on and on. Every one of these examples paints a clear picture of focusing on lack and scarcity.

If this describes your current situation, you may feel like arguing, "Well of COURSE I'm focused on those things - they are my reality right now!"

I know how difficult this suggestion is going to sound, but the fact remains that you will not be able to attract abundance into your life until you firmly turn your focus AWAY from lack and scarcity.

You have to begin focusing on SOME facet of abundance in order to draw more of it to you. There are many ways to do this, and we'll be covering many of them in the following pages of this book. But in a general sense, begin to develop an awareness of your focus from day to day. Start paying closer attention to the general direction of your thoughts and emotions regarding money.

How often do you catch yourself worrying, or feeling frustrated or fearful about money and bills? How often do you feel jealous, angry or resentful toward people who have a lot of money?

Once you start noticing these emotional responses within yourself, begin to turn them around deliberately.

For example, let's say you just caught yourself worrying whether you will have enough money to pay your monthly bills that are due next week. In the moment you become aware of this focus, you can CHOOSE to turn it around. Say to yourself, "I no longer need to worry about money. I always have more than enough money to cover everything I need."

At first you probably won't believe such a statement. In fact, I can practically guarantee you won't believe it immediately, because if you did your outer reality would reflect it. Even if you don't believe what you are saying, firmly set your doubt aside and keep saying the statement over and over again, day after day, and it will begin to sink into your subconscious mind.

Why is this important?

Because your subconscious beliefs trigger corresponding thoughts and feelings – which alter the frequency you emit to the universe, which attracts corresponding results back to you!

Another challenge with this strategy is that results may not show up immediately, leading you to believe that it's not working. Most of us tend to try something for a few days, maybe a week or two, then look at our outer environment to see if anything has changed. If not, we conclude it didn't work and give up. But I must stress that even if you don't see immediate results from this technique, keep doing it anyway! In fact, the long-term results you can achieve with this are far more profound than you can imagine. After a certain amount of time has passed (which will vary for everyone), you'll notice abundance in all forms showing up in greater amounts and frequencies in all areas of your life.

Do yourself a huge favor and decide to make this technique a lifelong habit rather than a short-term trial. Vow to keep up with it every day, day after day, for the rest of your life. Eventually you WILL see the results.

Finally, understand that you don't have to be perfect at this exercise for it to work. Don't make the mistake of thinking that a day or two of slipping back into scarcity thoughts will "undo" all of the work you've done. It doesn't work like that. In fact, if you can get yourself to the place of focusing on abundance more often than you focus on scarcity, you are ahead of the game! Granted, you want to do this as much as you possibly can, but even a good majority of the time will help a lot.

## #2 – Let Joy Be Your Copilot

Have you ever had one of those days where you just feel good for no particular reason? You woke up in a good mood and just felt lighthearted and cheerful all day long? If you think back to the last day you felt that way, you'll probably remember that everything seemed to flow easily for you. Even if an obstacle or two happened to pop up, you didn't let them get you down and probably found a way to skate right past them.

There's an important reason why days like this are so great – because JOY is your navigator! I'm not talking about just "happiness" here. Joy is a few notches above happiness on the emotional scale. When you feel happy, you are feeling good. When you feel joyful, you are feeling GREAT! Your mood is high and resilient. Nothing can get you down. You feel good about everyone and everything.

There are two reasons why you should try to get yourself into a joyful state of mind as often as possible: first, the emotion of joy emits a strong, high, positive frequency that can attract great things into your experience; and secondly, the emotion of joy keeps you highly RECEPTIVE to the good things flowing your way. In other words, you are open to receive. The longer you can stay in a joyful state of mind each day, the more miracles you will see happening around you.

But how do you get into this state purposely, let alone STAY in it?

There are endless ways to do it. Basically, consider for a moment the types of things that make you feel great. Maybe you love listening to great music. Or jogging. Or looking back through your childhood photo albums. Maybe reading inspiring books or watching emotionally stirring films works for you.

It doesn't matter how you get yourself into a joyful state, but the biggest challenge is CHOOSING to do so. As great as those random joyful days are, they don't happen often enough on their own. It's up to you to make them happen.

Start each day by thinking about, listening to, watching or reading material that will get your positive emotions flowing. Keep going until you feel ready to burst with joy and enthusiasm, and then let those feelings direct everything you do all day long.

Do what you love and love what you do! You can either spend time doing things that will keep your positive emotions going strong, or even if you have to do things you'd rather not, give your best effort into doing them joyfully. It's amazing how even the most unpleasant chores can be fun when we adopt the right mind-set!

Again, this is something you want to try to do daily, if you can. And again, don't worry about it if you have an off day here and there. You don't have to be perfect with this, just make an effort to be joyful as much as you can, and watch as your surroundings transform – including your financial state!

In fact, you can apply this strategy specifically to your financial situation and reap even greater rewards. Try getting into a joyful state just before you pay your bills. Feel great about the money you are sending out, and affirm confidently that more will be flowing in soon. Another thing you can do is write a check to yourself for a large amount of money, and spend time holding it and looking at it each day. Imagine that you really DID receive a large check, and the money is already yours. Allow yourself to get into a state of awe, joy and gratitude for your good fortune.

(Don't laugh – have you ever heard how superstar actor Jim Carrey wrote himself a check for $10 million several years ago? He now commands much more than that for every film he makes!)

There are many more ways to bring an element of joy into your financial situation and beyond; just get creative and have fun with it! The more positive emotion you can direct toward your financial situation overall, the quicker you will see positive changes taking place.

## #3 – *Stir Your Passion*

Just like joy, passion has the power to really get your juices flowing, so to speak - and that can also translate into a stronger and more powerful frequency. Think about the last time you did something you truly loved and how it made you feel. Didn't time seem to stop? Weren't you so immersed in the present that you forgot all about your troubles for a while?

This is why hobbies are so wonderful; they move us away from worry and stress into a more pleasant, peaceful state where we are totally connected to our inner selves. We so enjoy what we're doing that we forget about everything else. Worry, stress, fear, frustration – they all fade away and cease to exist for a period of time.

But how does this translate into increased abundance? Easy, when you're "in the flow" like that, ALL good things can come flowing to you more easily, and you are more receptive to allowing them into your life. In fact, joy and passion often go hand in hand: when you're joyful you're passionate and vice versa.

The problem is, who has time for hobbies? Most of us are extremely busy these days, rushing from the moment we wake up to the moment we fall into bed. You may not feel that you can afford the "luxury" of a hobby, but it's truly important to MAKE time for it. And it does not have to be long periods of time, either. Could you afford an hour or two a week? If even that short amount of time still seems doubtful, take a closer look at your weekly schedule and ask yourself if you really must do all the things you normally do. Can you carve out even a little time to indulge your passions?

If you truly can't manage a full hour, try 15 minutes and gradually increase to more.

(It's interesting to note that many people discover that when they start making time for their hobbies and interests, they begin to feel like the pace of their lives slows down, in turn making it seem like they have MORE time, not less. Try it yourself and see if you don't experience the same.)

The next question is what you should do with that time. You may already have a list of interests and hobbies to choose from, in which case, go for it! But if you don't know what your true passions and interests are, take some time to find out. Think about subjects and activities you've always wanted to learn more about and begin exploring them. Visit a craft supply store or even the library and browse around until you start to get some ideas.

Once you've decided on some activities, the final challenge will be pushing yourself to honor your commitment to spend time doing them. If you're like most people, you'll probably find yourself tempted to put it aside when you get busy or stressed, but try to avoid doing so because it is at times like that that you really NEED to do it. You need to get that passion stirred up and ignited as often as possible, so take your "me time" very seriously. Make a promise to yourself and stick to it, except in extreme emergencies.

What can you expect as you begin making your passions a priority?

You may be surprised! First of all, you'll feel happier. Those happy, passionate feelings will seep into your overall frequency and begin attracting great things back to you. For one, more time to indulge your passions! Like mentioned before, you'll probably find that time seems to slow down and you have more opportunity to spend time doing things you love. You may also find yourself enjoying your other normal activities more than you used to. You may attract new friends or romantic interests into your life. And yes, more money!

In fact, don't be surprised if wonderful things happen WHILE you are immersed in your passions, and the results can also linger for days afterward. Anything is possible. So pick up that paintbrush, fire up the piano, grab your camera (or whatever your chosen medium may be) and get those passionate feelings flowing.

## #4 – Gratitude Unlocks the Goodness

I'm sure you've heard it many times before, but the simple truth is that gratitude is one of the most powerful tools you have at your disposal. The reason why some people don't experience great results from a gratitude practice is usually because they aren't putting their full attention into it. Think of gratitude like a mirror that reflects back the same intensity that you put forth. Put a lot of emotion and power into it, get that same intensity of results back.

Feel a little grateful, get a little bit to be grateful for. Feel profoundly grateful . . . and watch in awe as one miracle after another comes zooming into your life.

The greatest thing about gratitude is that it usually does not take a long time to see results. If you can spend one whole day flowing strong, genuine feelings of gratitude toward everyone and everything in your life, that one day will change your entire life. You just won't believe all the great things you'll pull to yourself immediately.

In fact, that's one of the simplest ways to get started with a gratitude practice – just try it for one day! When you wake up in the morning, make a promise to yourself that you are going to be deeply grateful for all of the blessings in your life.

Start by thinking about the obvious things like your family, friends, job, vehicle, home, pets, and so on. However, don't just "think about" these things, but instead really focus your full attention on them and affirm how much they contribute to your life. Imagine how you would feel if they were taken away and allow yourself to feel waves of knee-weakening gratitude and appreciation for them being in your life.

As you move through your day, make it a point to give thanks for everything you see, touch, and experience. Even the "bad" stuff! Find one thing about every situation that you can be truly grateful for, and focus on that. Give thanks for your legs while you walk down the street. Give thanks for your lungs as you breathe. Give thanks for the food you eat and the beautiful world surrounding you, the people you meet, the experiences you have – everything!

Can you also see ways to apply this technique to your financial situation? Give heartfelt thanks for every penny you receive, every penny you give, and everything related to your abundance.

Once you give this technique an honest try, you'll probably make it a daily habit because you'll quickly realize how powerful it is. The key is to really FEEL the feelings of gratitude, not just think about them mentally. It may take some practice to fully master it, but once you do, it will change your life.

## #5 – *Visualize What You Want*

Visualization is yet another powerful tool you can use each day to help attract the things you want into your life. And it's so easy to do! The trick to making visualization work for you is to have FUN with it. Really allow yourself to get into the images you are seeing. Imagine how you will feel as you buy your dream home or a brand-new car. Imagine having pocketfuls of money to spend on whatever you like, and the sense of freedom that will come along with it. Imagine being able to give your close family and friends cash gifts, as well as beautiful things you would like to buy for them. Imagine taking fun vacations to exotic locations. Imagine paying your bills easily and on time. Imagine seeing a much larger balance in your bank account.

The great thing about visualizing is that you can really focus on any aspect of your new future that you like. For example, you can visualize money actually coming into your life by imagining that you are receiving checks in the mail, or by imagining yourself getting a great new job with a big salary. Or, you can imagine what your life will be like after you are already consistently receiving large sums of money on a regular basis and focus more on the lifestyle you will be living. Imagine yourself walking through the rooms of your beautiful new home, or relaxing on your gorgeous patio with a gourmet outdoor kitchen.

You can visualize your dream career, home life, social activities, or anything else you want to experience. You can zoom in on one particular aspect of a situation, or step back and see the big picture.

Visualization is like having your own private movie theatre in your mind! You can create and play as many movies as you like, and place yourself in the starring role.

Have fun with it. Don't treat it like a chore or requirement to getting what you want. In fact, going into it with a negative attitude is one way to be sure it won't work for you. On the other hand, if you can devote a strong level of positive emotion and lightheartedness to the process, you will be amazed at how well it works – and how good it makes you feel even before your chosen experiences show up in your physical surroundings!

## #6 – *That's Affirmative*

Affirmations are another powerful tool that can help shift your mind-set to one of greater abundance and joy. The trick to using affirmations effectively is twofold: constant repetition and strong, positive emotion!

Affirmations work directly on your subconscious mind and help change old, ingrained beliefs. However, remember that a belief is simply a thought you have repeated to yourself over and over again, so it becomes your "truth." Consequently, it may take a little time to change those old limiting beliefs to something better.

For example, let's say you begin reciting the affirmation, "I attract abundance easily." If you have spent much of your lifetime focused on lack and scarcity, your subconscious mind will resist this new thought because it feels like a lie. Your subconscious mind is constantly repeating the beliefs, "I do not have enough money. I can't get ahead. I always pay my bills late. My credit cards are maxed out," and so on.

And indeed, this may be the reality you see as you look at your outer life. But it's important to understand that your outer circumstances are the direct RESULT of your inner beliefs. Whether these beliefs were given to you by other people (for example, your parents) or whether you created them yourself, you'll need to overwrite those old beliefs with new ones. And doing that may take some time.

The good news is that if you keep repeating thoughts like, "I attract abundance easily. I always have more than enough money. Money comes to me from many different sources," and so on, your subconscious mind will begin to believe them, and your outer circumstances will begin to shift to support your new beliefs.

Even more importantly, infusing the process with strong, positive emotion will give your affirmations that much more power. For example, reciting the words, "I always have more than enough money for everything I need" while also feeling happy and peaceful inside delivers the "truth" of this statement directly to your subconscious mind. Why? Because your subconscious mind CANNOT tell the difference between something you are really experiencing, and something you are imagining. When you feel strong emotion and think repetitive thoughts, your subconscious mind absorbs the messages.

Ironically, this is exactly how lack and scarcity beliefs are formed too! You think thoughts like these: "I never have enough money. Making enough money to get by is really hard. I always have to struggle for the things I want..." – and at the same time you are flowing tons of negative emotions. Consequently, your subconscious mind says, "This must be true."

The good news is that you have conscious control over what you think and feel. You may be in the habit of thinking and feeling negatively, but you can change it at any time! Just remember that it is a process, so be sure to give it time.

## #7 – *Putting on a New Persona*

As I said earlier, you may feel like you are lying to yourself at the beginning. When you first begin using affirmations or visualizations (or any other tool), you may feel a twinge of discomfort, like you are wearing someone else's clothing. It just doesn't seem to feel right. You may feel minor discomfort or stronger emotions like disbelief, restlessness, embarrassment, or even impatience.

That's because you are challenging your existing beliefs! That's your subconscious mind saying, "Hey, wait a minute, this isn't the reality I know. This puzzle piece doesn't fit with all the rest."

Some people will stop using the technique at this point because they think it's not working. Don't do that! When you start feeling that strangeness, it's a good sign that you are pushing some hot buttons in your subconscious mind. You are challenging long-standing beliefs that do not serve you, and you can override them if you keep going.

To help this process along, you may want to practice putting on your new persona each day for a few minutes (or longer if you can). Take a moment to think about who you are right now. You have a mental image of yourself that matches the way you look, the things you do, and your circumstances in life.

Now think about the things you want to attract into your life, like more money, a better job or booming business, better relationships, a new residence, and so on. Are you currently the type of person who would slide seamlessly into that type of setting? Can you really see yourself living in a huge house, driving fancy cars or having the type of career you want?

You may have some difficulty fitting your current self-image into the new circumstances you desire, and that is normal. Most people will experience this simply because they haven't yet developed into the person who would comfortably fit with the reality they desire. They are more comfortable with their current reality because they've been living it for years.

However, you can easily "try on" your new reality by mentally stepping into the shoes of the person you will be in your new circumstances. For example, if you are trying to attract a larger sum of money to have in the bank, periodically throughout the day imagine what it feels like to have that size bank account. You might say to yourself, "Wow, that's right, I have $50,000 in my bank account right now." And then allow yourself to FEEL as if you really do. Does that thought change your perception of yourself at all? Does it make your step a little lighter, your shoulders pull back a little bit more? Do you feel a little less stressed?

The first several times you do this, don't be surprised if you feel weird about it. Your subconscious mind will be screaming, "You are such a liar! You know you don't have that kind of money! Who do you think you're fooling?" Don't listen to it. Either ignore that little voice, or have fun with it. You might reply mentally, "Ah, but I WILL have a lot more money one day very soon. I know it's coming and I'm just trying it on for size."

The greatest thing about this technique is that it works even if you know you are "lying." It does not prevent you from pretending or acting as if you already have what you want. And as you emit the thoughts and feelings of someone who already has what they want, you begin to draw it to you!

Even if you feel strange doing this, make it a point to do it anyway, at least once a day. It does get easier the more you do it, and it can actually be a lot of fun!

Here are a few more ideas to help you make it seem like a fun game:

- After driving somewhere, get out of your car while pretending it's a chauffeured limousine. Imagine you are stepping out onto a red carpet, wearing designer clothing and smiling for cameras. Even if you have no desire to be famous, have fun playing with the idea and I guarantee you'll be laughing in no time.

- As you are shopping in stores, pretend that you have enough money to buy anything you desire. Walk up and down the aisles thinking to yourself, "Wow, I could buy everything they have on the shelves and STILL not run out of money!" Pretend you are shopping for expensive gifts for your friends and family. Or pretend you are buying a whole new wardrobe for yourself, or stocking your kitchen with the best gourmet foods and culinary gadgets.

- When you go to sleep at night, imagine that you are lying in your dream bed in your dream house. Mentally think about what your dream bedroom looks like and pretend that you are there now. (This is so easy to do if you close your eyes!) Then allow your mind to travel out of your bedroom and into the hall, and move throughout the rest of your dream home, taking note of what it all looks like. How does it feel to be there? Enjoy it! The more "real" you can make it, the more power you lend to the actual creation of it.

The more you "put on" this new persona and step into your new life circumstances, the more easily your subconscious mind will begin to accept a new reality – and the more easily you'll be able to attract it.

## #8 – *Transform Your Core Beliefs*

We touched on beliefs briefly in the section on affirmations, but there are other beliefs that will make it nearly impossible for you to achieve any lasting level of change in your life if you don't also address them, and those are your "core beliefs."

Your core beliefs are the ones that shape your entire view of reality. Most of these beliefs began forming when you were very young, and you have continued to reinforce them throughout your life.

Let's look at an example core belief regarding money.

If you grew up in a household where your parents worked very hard and earned just enough money to survive, you would probably hold strong beliefs that it's hard to make money and you don't need very much to get by. For a person with this type of belief, scarcity and frugality would seem normal, and the concept of "wealth" (having much more than you actually need for basic survival) would be foreign and perhaps even uncomfortable.

I chose this belief as our example purposely because it's so common. Most of the people reading this book likely come from hard-working, low- to middle-class families. How do I know that? Easy. Someone who comes from a wealth-conscious environment probably wouldn't be reading this book at all. Attracting abundance would be completely natural to them because they would have the beliefs that support such a reality.

With a core belief based on scarcity such as this one, affirmations and visualization may not be effective enough to see any change. It's like trying to convince yourself that you are tall when you are actually short, or that you are a woman when you are actually a man, and so on. A core belief is such a deep part of who you are that changing it will take a bit more effort.

There are different ways to transform your core beliefs, and not all of them will work for everyone. You may need to try several approaches before you find one that works for you, but most likely all of them will take some time to see results, so be sure to stay with a practice for a month or two before determining whether it is working or not.

Here some options for addressing your core beliefs:

### • Hypnosis

Hypnosis is very effective because it works with your subconscious mind directly. The hypnotherapist is able to get you to relax completely so your natural defenses are down, and then help you record new beliefs that will override the old ones. Some people may need only one session for a new belief to take root, while others may need several visits. You can also try self-hypnosis if you don't want to work with a therapist. There are many audio programs that address different kinds of core beliefs, including financial ones. Again, you may need to use the audio program multiple times before it begins to work.

### • EFT or other "clearing" process

Many people report good results using EFT (Emotional Freedom Techniques) to clear limiting beliefs. EFT works on the pressure points of your body's energy lines (called meridians). You simply recite key phrases while tapping firmly on specific points on your body and clear blockages in your energy field. Some practitioners report immediate improvement, while others report the need for consistent usage over time. You could also try other clearing processes like acupuncture, acupressure, chakra balancing, and so on.

### • Sheer repetition

As I said earlier, most of your core beliefs were formed years ago, but they were formed in the same way all your other beliefs were formed: by thinking specific kinds of thoughts over and over again until they became cemented in your subconscious as "truth."

To change those beliefs, you simply need to get into the habit of thinking better thoughts. Use the same process described in the section on affirmations: recite empowering phrases that you want to be true, while also feeling strong, positive emotions about them.

Here's a good way to tell whether you are having an effect on your core beliefs:

Write a list of statements that you believe to be true. For example, "Everything always goes wrong for me. I have a hard time making money. I can't seem to get ahead financially." Then carefully pay attention to how you feel when you say these statements to yourself. Do they feel true to you? When you first get started, they probably will. That means you do believe them. As you work on changing your core beliefs, you'll begin to notice that reciting those statements triggers a feeling of doubt or resistance. They no longer seem to be completely true anymore.

Now you can write more empowering beliefs like these: "I'm really lucky. Money comes to me easily. I receive money from many different sources." As you work on changing your core beliefs, these positive statements will begin to feel more real to you. Saying them will resonate with you and they will feel like truth. That means you are creating core beliefs that these new things are true, and that means you will have a much easier time attracting experiences that support them!

## #9 – Check Your Expectations

Have you ever caught yourself expecting the worst? Maybe before a job interview you got caught up in thoughts like, "What if I screw up the interview? They probably won't hire me anyway; there must be better candidates for the job."

Or when you set a big goal and begin moving toward it, you may find yourself thinking things like, "This doesn't seem to be working, I'm not getting the results I want. This is probably a waste of time, like everything else I try to do."

Expectations hold a lot of power! In fact, they are equally as powerful as your beliefs. In general, what you expect, you get. The question is, what do you usually expect?

Do you expect to have trouble paying your bills each month? Do you expect things to go wrong for you? Do you expect to be left out, ridiculed or rejected?

If you take a moment to think back through your memorable life experiences, you can probably come up with plenty of examples of when your expectations hopped into the driver's seat and brought about exactly the outcome you were expecting.

The good news is that you can use this same power to deliberately choose something better.

With every situation you face, ask yourself which outcome you would like to experience. Then EXPECT it to happen that way.

For example, while working toward a goal, keep repeating, "I just know this is going to work out perfectly." Or when you feel nervous about an interview, affirm several times, "This is going to be great, I'm going to give it my best shot and get the job easily."

Do the same thing with your finances. Expect to be wealthy. Expect to be abundant in all areas. Expect money and great opportunities to come to you easily. Expect to be able to pay your bills easily. Expect to be able to buy the things you want.

The more you get in the habit of expecting the best, the more you'll find yourself receiving it!

At the same time, you can also use this strategy when you find yourself overcome with negative expectations. When you notice that you are adopting a pessimistic mind-set, immediately stop yourself and turn around your thoughts. Example: If you just caught yourself thinking, "I don't know why I keep trying to improve my financial situation, it's just not working!" Stop and say, "I may not have seen big results yet, but I know that all this effort is going to pay off soon. Any time now I expect to receive clear confirmation that things are turning around in my favor."

Again, this may take time to work completely, but the more you do it the more quickly you'll see results.

## #10 – Giving from Joy

You've probably heard that giving is another powerful way to attract more abundance into your life, but there are certain ways to do it that work better than others.

First, you don't want to give for the purpose of receiving, or with an expectation that you will receive within a certain timeframe. The purpose of giving should be that it makes you feel good. The better it makes you feel to give, the more of a return you will receive.

Giving from joy accomplishes two things:

First, it makes you feel really good when you give in a way that is meaningful to you. Giving to a cause that matters to you, helping someone who desperately needs it, or even giving anonymously are all great ways to get those good vibes flowing and trigger a return response from the universe.

Secondly, when you give like this you are sending a clear message of abundance to the universe. You are saying, "I have plenty of money, so I joyfully share it with others." The universe hears, "I have plenty of money and I love sharing it, so please send me more to enjoy and share" – and begins to shift your physical circumstances so that you DO have plenty of money to enjoy and share!

However, note that this process also can take time to grow and develop in your life, especially if you have spent years thinking about giving to others but holding back because you didn't feel you had enough.

If it makes you more comfortable, start giving small amounts but imagine that they are bigger and allow yourself to feel like you would if you were giving a sizeable donation. When you write a check for $5, imagine that it's $500. If you drop a dollar into a tip jar, pretend it's a $100 bill, and imagine the look of surprise and delight on the face of the person who receives it.

You can also do this in other ways besides financially. Be generous with your time and energy, with your support and encouragement, and with your love. As you share these qualities with others each day, affirm and know that the universe is sending more of the same right back to you.

## #11 – Peace in Abundance

Your emotional state on a day-to-day basis has a powerful effect on your overall financial picture. When you think about the way the Law of Attraction really works, you know that your thoughts, feelings and beliefs all contribute to your energy "frequency" that is sent to the universe. The universe then responds by sending corresponding situations and events that match your frequency.

What is your emotional state like most of the time? Do you constantly feel stressed about money? Do you spend much of each day worried and anxious about paying your bills? Do you focus obsessively on your empty bank account or wallet? These emotional reactions will keep perpetuating the cycle of lack in your life, because your frequency is "asking" for much of the same!

On the other hand, consider how you would feel day to day if you had plenty of money in the bank. Would you be anxious or fearful? Would you be worrying about how to pay your bills at the end of the month? No. You'd feel just the opposite. You'd feel peaceful about money. Your whole financial attitude would be calm and positive.

In fact, money would be a non-issue for you and you'd hardly think about money at all! You'd focus on your day-to-day activities with the inner knowledge that all is well in your financial world. In other words, you'd move through each day with a core of inner peace.

You can do the same thing NOW. When you begin altering your emotional state like this purposely, you alter the frequency you send to the universe. The universe then alters your physical surroundings to match!

One of the quickest and easiest ways to attract great abundance into your life is to think, feel and act as if you already have what you want.

Beginning right now, spend a few minutes each day feeling the way you would feel if you already had plenty of money. Imagine the figure you want to have in your bank account, and get into the feeling place of such a reality. If you like, you can use some positive self-talk to help you along. For example, say something like, "It feels so good to be financially secure. I love knowing that I have plenty of money to cover my needs. All is well in my world, and I'm so grateful for that."

This will take practice at the beginning, but eventually you'll start to notice a different feeling take over your body. Your muscles will loosen, you'll feel yourself calming down and feeling more relaxed and peaceful. Before long, you will reach a point where you know that you DO have plenty of money at your disposal, even though it hasn't yet shown up in your physical world. You'll know it's coming soon, though. It will feel natural to imagine more money in your bank account and wallet. And of course, if you master this technique, it probably won't be long before you really DO have the money you desire.

Even better, you can use this technique in other areas of your life besides money, and it will still have a positive effect on your financial situation! For example, if you usually feel stressed at work, make it a point to purposely let go of stressful thoughts and feelings and pretend that you are calm and peaceful. Do the same with your relationships, health, social activities and more.

Become a vessel for peace and well-being, and that feeling will transform all areas of your life.

## #12 – Reinforce the Positive

It's frightening how easy it is to get into a lack-focused state of mind and end up attracting more of the same!

How many times have you done something like this? You get an unexpected bill that you don't have the money to pay immediately, and it sends you into a tailspin of worry and fear. First you start worrying that you won't be able to pay the unexpected bill, but before you know it, you're worrying about other things that might break down or go wrong, or you may even start worrying about the security of your job and the general state of your financial well-being – all because you received one unexpected bill.

This can be a frightening situation to be in for sure, but moving into a state of worry and fear will only make things worse. In fact, you can probably remember plenty of times when you began worrying about one thing and before long found that more and more things started going wrong.

The good news is that it works in reverse too!

Rather than worrying when something seems to go wrong, turn it into something positive! Remember that your thoughts and emotions can pull all kinds of miracles into your life if you will just stay open to receiving them. There are many ways to do this, but here are a few simple ways you can begin reinforcing the positive starting today.

### • Get excited.

When you receive an unexpected bill that you can't pay right away, or even if you are struggling to pay your regular expenses each month, get into a state of excitement and happiness about it and use it as an opportunity to attract more money. Rather than worrying, "How am I going to pay this bill?" affirm and know that you will receive the money to pay it easily. Say to yourself, "Cool! I've got a bill here for $498, so that means I will soon be receiving that sum or more! My bills are always paid easily and on time, and this one will be too. Thank you!" Allow yourself to FEEL exactly as you would if you knew you always had plenty of money to cover your expenses and more. Then put it out of your mind and act as if it was already a done deal; the bill is already paid in full. When you do this consistently, you will be telling the universe, "I always have more than enough money for everything I need." In turn, the universe will mirror exactly that reality, over and over again.

- **Focus on what you receive.**

Most of us focus obsessively on the "negatives," like bills that must be paid, but we rarely focus on the "positives," like the money we receive from various sources. For example, when you receive your paycheck, how do you feel about it? Do you focus on whether it will be enough? Do you resent the fact that much of it will be sent to creditors? Do you feel that you are underpaid or underappreciated for what you do? How about when you receive some unexpected money? Do you feel grateful and blessed, or do you focus on what you still don't have? Get into the habit of emitting strong, positive emotion about every penny you receive, and watch in amazement as more and more begins to flow into your life.

- **Open to opportunities.**

Another way many of us focus on the negative is by holding a very narrow view of the possibilities for more abundance. We think that there are only a few limited ways that we can receive money –like through a job or business – and consequently we block out all other possibilities! A great way to turn this around is by affirming each day that you have unlimited opportunities to receive greater abundance. Say out loud or mentally, "Wow, I can receive money and other forms of abundance in so many ways. The universe is going to surprise me with some great opportunities today!" Or you can say, "I am always in the right place at the right time to receive abundance." Any affirmation along these lines will work great to help you expand your focus so you will indeed be more open to opportunities.

## #13 – Laugh all the way to the bank.

Laughter is one of the most powerful tools you have for attracting abundance into your life. That may sound ridiculous, but it is so powerful once you understand why it works. As you know, your thoughts and emotions are what the Law of Attraction is responding to. In other words, your thoughts and emotions are "asking" for specific types of experiences, whether you know it or not. How do you feel when you are laughing and having a good time? You feel lighthearted, joyful, free and . . . well, just plain GOOD! That mental and emotional state begins immediately pulling corresponding situations into your life, including greater abundance.

Likewise, when you feel down, sad, irritable, stressed and other negative emotions, your mental and emotional state is pulling similar situations back to you.

The greatest thing about laughter is that you don't have to focus on any particular thing in order to attract goodness in ALL forms. You can be laughing at a silly movie or television show, and you're subconsciously sending a signal to the universe that says, "I feel good, send me more good things."

However, you can drastically improve your results in attracting more abundance by focusing on your financial situation while you are feeling joyful and happy. Here's an easy way to do it.

Set aside time to laugh at least once each day, but more often is better. To do this you'll need to watch or read something funny, spend time having fun with friends or family, or even just think about something funny if you have a creative imagination. You want to spend at least 10 to 15 minutes laughing and feeling really good. While you are doing so, send out a few strong, positive thoughts about your financial situation.

For example, while you're laughing, think to yourself, "Wow, I'm feeling really optimistic about all areas of my life, especially money. I know things are going to turn around for me. More money is flowing to me right now. I am pulling unlimited abundance into my life right now!" Or you can call up a mental image of your bank account balance being bigger, see yourself paying your bills easily, and so on. The exact thoughts do not matter, except that they are positive, optimistic and related directly to your financial situation.

Even better, you don't have to worry about "how" you will make all this stuff happen. Much of the time it will happen spontaneously. Either you'll receive money from unexpected sources, or great opportunities will seem to drop right into your lap. You may also meet new people that will lead to you greater abundance opportunities. The possibilities are truly endless. But they ALL start by shifting into a more positive, joyful state of mind, and laughter is a big key to doing that.

## *#14 – Talk yourself up.*

Throughout the pages of this book, I've mentioned several examples of positive self-talk but self-talk can be so powerful that it deserves a section of its own. In fact, you may be surprised to discover that much of your outer circumstances are the direct result of the things you say to yourself on a regular basis!

We all talk to ourselves, sometimes mentally and sometimes verbally. We talk ourselves through problems ("What can I do to turn this around?"), remind ourselves about chores and tasks we need to do ("Don't forget to buy milk on the way home."), and even more importantly, we use self-talk to shape our perception of reality.

Self-talk is powerful because it automatically triggers corresponding emotional states and sets you up with specific expectations.

Have you ever caught yourself saying things like, "It figures that something had to go wrong, that always happens to me!" Or, "I don't know why I bother to keep trying to improve my life, I'm never going to be successful."

Statements like those are extremely illuminating if you pay attention to them because they usually reveal deep-seated beliefs about yourself, your life in general, and your day-to-day expectations.

If you have gotten into the habit of engaging in regular negative self-talk, you are actually drawing more similar circumstances to yourself. In other words, you're ASKING for them!

But just like negative self-talk can become a mindless habit, so can positive self-talk! That's right: you can actually set yourself up to automatically attract great things into your life, including more money and abundance in all forms.

The way to do it is incredibly simple: start talking more positively to and about yourself!

You're probably not even aware of it, but you have an ongoing mental conversation running every minute of every day. For the majority of people, it probably sounds something like this: "My life is so challenging. Nothing ever works out for me. I don't have enough money. I struggle to pay my bills on time. I'm sick of struggling for everything. I'm sick of working so hard and getting nowhere. Other people have it so easy and I have it so hard. It's not fair. Life isn't fair ..." I could go on, but you get the picture.

What do you think would happen if these people were able to change their mental conversation to sound something more like this: "Wow, I am so blessed! Life is so great. I've got so much to be grateful for. Good things happen to me constantly. I've got so many wonderful opportunities available to me. I trust my instincts and I'm always led to the best possible outcomes. I've got so much abundance in every area of my life. I deserve all of the good things I want. Life is good. I love my life!"

Does this sound too "Pollyanna-ish" to you? Does it seem like a person who thinks like this must be living in a fantasy world? Believe it or not, there are plenty of people who not only think this way, but also live their entire lives with such a positive, powerful attitude. And even more importantly, the circumstances of their lives reflect it! They are indeed blessed, or what many of us would call "lucky." They have plenty of money, great friends, rewarding careers, abundant health, and much more. They constantly attract great experiences by default. They don't even have to think much about it; their mental and emotional state acts like a magnet for joy.

And you can do the same thing for yourself. Even better, you don't have to turn into a "Pollyanna" for this to work. In fact, if you can be positive just a little bit more than you are negative, you'll still see some improvements in your life! Make it your mission to simply attempt to be more positive with your self-talk every day, and then gradually increase your effort so that you will eventually be almost fully positive, and you'll still be able to make great progress.

The simplest way to start is by setting aside a few minutes first thing in the morning to think and speak positively and get yourself into a good state of mind for the day. Very often, the whole theme of your day will be based on the thoughts you think first thing in the morning. If you wake up grumpy and irritable, chances are the whole day will go that way. Likewise, when you wake up happy and lighthearted.

When you first wake up in the morning, go into the bathroom and look at yourself in the mirror. Greet yourself like you would a good friend. You can grin and say, "Hi there! How are you today?" Then continue by saying positive things to and about yourself and your life. For example, "You're looking good today. You are a good person, you know that? You deserve everything good you desire, and you are going to attract it all easily and quickly, starting today! In fact, today is going to be a fantastic day. Everything is going to go your way today, just wait and see. Go get 'em, and remember, you are loved!"

Don't laugh – it really does work! At first you may feel pretty silly saying these things to yourself, but within a few days you should be feeling lighthearted and humorous about the whole thing. (On second thought, go ahead and laugh all you want because you'll just be adding more positive vibes to your frequency!)

Before you go to sleep, say a few positive things about yourself. For example, "You know, (name), I am really proud of the way you handled that situation at work today. You could have freaked out but you kept your cool and it all came out fine. You rock!"

Or during the course of your day you can build yourself up by saying things like, "I'm really good at my job, and I love the feeling of satisfaction I get when I complete a project." Or, "I'm learning and growing more each day and I know that each day from here on out is going to be even better!"

Finally, you can also use this same process to think more positively about your life circumstances. Try saying things like this as often as you can: "I really love my life. Life is so good. I am so lucky! I've got so much to be grateful for ..." and so on.

In short, positive self-talk works on two important levels. First, it sets you up with positive expectations for your life experiences, and secondly, it gets those positive emotions flowing! The two of those combined are a sure recipe for abundance and success in all areas of your life.

## #15 – *Take one step forward each day.*

Have you noticed that the majority of the tips in this book are geared toward altering your mental and emotional state? There's an important reason for that: your mind and emotions are where all creation starts! If you don't first get your mind and feelings in line with what you want, all the action in the world won't do much to help you. You can probably think of plenty of people who work ridiculously hard and still have very little to show for it. Maybe you are even one of those people. I used to be, so I know what a frustrating place that is to be.

However, action is not such a bad thing either, and in fact, it can be a great help in getting things moving in a better direction.

So, while you are focusing on improving your thoughts and choosing more positive emotions and expectations, you may also want to begin taking action on just one thing each day that will help you to improve your financial situation. It does not have to be a BIG action – just something to begin moving you in the direction you want to go.

Right now, take a few minutes to jot down a list of 10 things you could do to help improve your financial situation immediately. Ideas might include selling something you no longer need, applying for a better job, starting a savings plan, investing money for long-term growth, going back to school for more career training, getting a part-time job to pay down debt, starting your own business, having a yard sale, and so on.

The whole point of action steps like these is NOT to try to change everything yourself, but rather to make you feel more empowered as you begin moving toward what you want. As you begin taking at least one step in that direction every day, you'll usually find that each consecutive step seems easier and easier, and before long, momentum takes over. Before you know it, you're making huge changes in your life and feeling great about it.

Another kind of action you'll definitely want to take is inspired action – that is, when you feel you are being nudged to do something specific by the universe. For example, you might suddenly feel inspired to call a friend you haven't spoken to in a while, or take a different route home from work one day, or request information on a particular career option – and it will be exactly the right move to open up a new world of possibility for you.

It's hard to give examples of inspired actions because the actions themselves might seem inconsequential. But you'll always know because you'll just "feel" that you should do something specific. When you get that feeling, definitely follow through with it! More often than not it will lead you to something great.

## #16 – Be okay with money flowing OUT.

Not only should you focus on attracting more money to flow IN, it's also just as important to alter your thoughts and feelings about the money you spend. Think for a moment about how you view spending right now. Do you avoid spending money because you're afraid you won't have enough to cover your bills each month? Do you spend TOO

MUCH to pacify an emotional need? Do you feel resentful about the money you send to your landlord or mortgage company, creditors and service suppliers?

The way you view spending can have a dramatic impact on your overall level of abundance. If you have unhealthy spending habits (whether excessive spending or excessive scrimping), you are effectively blocking more money from coming into your life.

Think about that for a moment. If you resent sending money to people and companies that have loaned you money or provided services to you, you are attracting more opportunities to resent sending money out! If you spend recklessly in order to fill an emotional need, you are attracting more emotional emptiness that you'll have to try to fill! If you are afraid to spend money because you are afraid you won't have enough money to cover your basic expenses, you will simply attract more situations where you don't have enough!

It sounds overly simple, but it really does work that way where the Law of Attraction is concerned.

So what IS a healthy spending attitude?

Quite simply, you want to strike a healthy balance between spending confidently yet responsibly, while always knowing that you have more than enough money coming in. You don't want to spend excessively, but you don't want to restrict your spending unnecessarily either.

This does take practice to master and it can seem

overwhelming at times, especially if you have had unhealthy spending habits for any length of time. However, turning them around is fairly simple with a little conscious awareness. Here's how to start:

- Begin appreciating the people and companies you send money to each month. Flow deep feelings of appreciation to your mortgage company or landlord when you write out your monthly check to them. In your heart thank them for helping to put a stable roof over your head, and affirm that you are glad to send money to them for that gift. Do the same when you write checks to service suppliers like the electric company, gas company, oil company, cable television, Internet provider, and so on. Take a moment to reflect on how grateful you are to enjoy the luxury of these services (for they are indeed luxuries that many people don't have), and affirm that you are grateful for the opportunity to pay for these luxuries each month. Do this same thing when you pay for repairs and maintenance on your home and vehicle!

- Share money with others. Even if you are in severe financial shortage right now, begin giving some money to charitable organizations, even if it's only $1 per month! When you give that money, feel grateful and happy that you have more than enough to share with others. This may seem like it would be depressing, but it is depressing ONLY if you focus on the fact that you can't afford to give more. If you instead focus on the positive and affirm that your money is going to a worthwhile cause, you can't help but feel GOOD about that, and end up attracting back more money.

- Spend money confidently when necessary. Have you ever avoided buying something that you really needed because you were trying to restrict your spending? It's one thing to restrict unnecessary spending, but quite another to avoid buying things you really need! The message you send to the universe when you do this is one that you do NOT want to be mirrored back in your life: that you don't have enough money for everything you need. It's no big surprise why you don't have enough money for everything you need if you regularly avoid spending with this mind-set! To turn this around, simply spend your money when you need to, and affirm confidently that the universe will make it all come out okay. This takes a big leap of faith sometimes, but true miracles can happen when you do it.

In short, you want to gradually get yourself into the state of mind where spending is okay because you know you will always have more money flowing in. That doesn't mean you should max out your credit cards and buy a bunch of things you don't really need; that just creates more problems down the road. But little by little convince yourself that you don't have to pinch pennies because more money is coming to you soon. You'll be surprised to see that the more you believe this, the more often it ends up being absolutely true!

## *#17 – Create a space for abundance.*

What kind of shape is your financial situation in? I don't mean whether you have enough money coming in, but whether it is ordered or chaotic. When was the last time you balanced your checkbook? Do you have a lot of expenses that are no longer necessary? Is your filing system up to date, or do you have stacks of unpaid bills and/or unfiled paperwork strewn about? Do you know exactly how much debt you have? Do you have a solid savings and investment plan in place?

I have mentioned several times throughout this book that focusing on lack is a bad thing, but that does not mean you should stick your head in the sand and refuse to acknowledge your current reality. In fact, I think you'll be pleased to discover that getting your financial affairs organized will create a big space into which abundance can flow!

There are three major steps to this process:

1) Clear out stagnation.

The first step is to clear away anything that could create a blockage for the abundance you wish to attract into your life. This includes throwing away paperwork that is no longer needed, clearing off your desk or the area in which you pay bills, and eliminating money drains like old subscriptions and memberships you no longer use.

2) Organize what's left.

Then, get organized in every area of your financial life. File away old paperwork that needs to be kept. Balance your checkbook and reconcile all of your financial accounts. Figure out exactly how much debt you have and set up a plan for paying it down, create a savings and investment plan if you don't already have one, and so on. There are two reasons why getting organized is so important: first, it helps you to see clearly where you are now, and compare it to where you want to be; and secondly, it makes you feel more empowered and in control. They say "ignorance is bliss" but not when it comes to financial issues! Rather than fearing how much debt you have, figure it out so you know for sure and you can take steps to reduce it. Likewise with how much money you have in the bank, and how much you would like to have.

3) Organize the rest of your life.

Since this book is about attracting abundance, I started with that area. But once that's done, you will also want to carry these same actions into other areas of your life. Clear out any material possessions you no longer need. Organize what you want to keep. Get rid of drains on your time and energy the same way, like canceling old commitments you no longer wish to keep, and so on.

Once again, this helps you feel more in control of your circumstances, which will trigger a more peaceful state of mind, and attract more experiences that support your intentions.

*Bonus Tip #18 – Start small!*

I have to include one more tip for you, simply because it may save you a lot of frustration and wasted energy.

When many people first learn about the Law of Attraction and try attracting more money into their lives, they usually go right for the big money. They set an intention to win $10 million in the lottery, or otherwise receive an exceedingly large amount of money.

It's not that attracting these things is impossible. They are definitely possible. But the problem arises when people try to take a massive leap from where they are to where they want to be, rather than learning how to crawl before they walk.

If you have been struggling financially for years, it's unrealistic to try to attract millions of dollars right out of the gate. You are likely to have MUCH more success if you take GRADUAL steps to where you want to be. And the best way to do that is to start small.

Take a moment to consider how much money you typically earn in a month right now, and then set a goal to attract that sum or only slightly more. If you want to really challenge yourself, set a goal to attract double or triple the amount of money you typically have. But avoid going much higher than that, simply because it will seem too unbelievable to you.

Once you are successfully attracting modest sums of money, you can simply keep raising the bar and attracting bigger and bigger amounts. And eventually, attracting a few million dollars will seem like a piece of cake.

*Conclusion*

As you can see from the tips shared in this section, attracting abundance is more a process of inner mastery and growth than anything else. The more abundant and empowered you feel on the inside, the more abundance you'll see in your outer reality – and it will be a very natural process; no struggle or strain involved.

The most challenging part for most people will be remembering to change the direction of their thoughts and gain control over their emotional responses. But like all habits, consistent effort will go a long way in creating long-term progress.

Be patient with yourself throughout your journey to abundance. Relax and have fun with it, and before you know it you'll realize that you are surrounded by goodness in all forms.

# SECTION III

# WHAT TO DO WHEN THE LAW OF ATTRACTION ISN'T WORKING

## *How to Clear Resistance and Work in Harmony with the Universe*

Discovering the Law of Attraction is one of the most inspiring and empowering moments in a person's life. No matter what kind of struggles and problems they have experienced in the past or may be experiencing right now, they suddenly feel confident that they can transform their lives and start anew.

Unfortunately for many people, that "honeymoon" phase doesn't last long. They may spend a few weeks, or perhaps months, trying to work with the Law of Attraction, make little progress, and eventually give up and resign themselves to living a less-than-optimal life.

But it doesn't have to be that way! The Law of Attraction is always at work, whether you believe it or not – and learning how to make it work in your favor is much easier than many people realize. There are some common mistakes that can throw a wrench into the whole process, however, and this guide is going to highlight those mistakes and offer simple solutions for them to help you improve your success with the Law of Attraction.

Better still, you should know that even if you have struggled to get the Law of Attraction to work for you, you probably are not far off in achieving success. You may simply be doing one or two small things that are enough to upset the whole process. Fix those, and progress resumes.

By the time you finish reading this guide you should have a solid understanding of exactly what to do (and what you should never do) to manifest anything you desire.

## *How the Law of Attraction Works*

The Law of Attraction operates according to your thoughts, feelings, and beliefs. Let's break down each component of the process:

**Thoughts**

Your thoughts are the beginning part of the creation process, and this aspect is all about focus. Simply stated, you get what you focus on the most. However, you don't have to focus on specific things in order to manifest them – just focusing on situations and experiences that are on the same energetic "frequency" is enough.

For example, focusing on negative things most of the time will continue to attract more negative experiences into your life. Focusing on positive things most of the time will continue to attract more positive experiences into your life.

Unfortunately, most of us have formed a bad habit of focusing on negative stuff far more often than we focus on the positive.

Do you have this habit also? Instead of focusing on something good that you would like to experience, do you complain about the unpleasant aspects of what you are experiencing now? Instead of choosing to see the positive side of a situation, do you focus on the drawbacks and problems instead?

It works the same way when you're trying to manifest something specific. You might be verbally asking the universe for more money – but then spend all day complaining about not having enough money, or constantly saying, "I can't afford that; I don't have enough money for that; I'm so tired of being broke." In this case you are actually focusing on the LACK of money, not having more money.

Do you see why some people think the Law of Attraction doesn't work? They may say, "I focus on money constantly but I still don't have any!" They are focusing on the feeling of not having enough money instead of having plenty of money. The energetic frequencies of those two conditions are drastically different.

**Feelings**

Your dominant emotional state also adds another element of power to the equation. Every thought triggers a corresponding emotion, which acts as fuel that propels your "request" to the universe – even if you are "asking" for something you don't want by focusing on it.

So when you think about how much you would love to find your soul mate, and you are filled with the emotions of love, joy, and contentment as you think about him or her, you communicate a message to the universe that you would love to meet him or her soon – and he or she begins moving toward you energetically and eventually physically.

But when you feel frustrated that you can't seem to meet your soul mate, you are filled with the emotions of sadness, loneliness and desperation, and you communicate a message that you'll probably never meet him or her and you are miserable because of it. And when you communicate this message of misery, you are only aligned with receiving more experiences that make you feel miserable.

**Beliefs**

Belief plays an equally important goal in the creation process as your thoughts and feelings, because your beliefs form the framework of what you will allow into your life – or not. If you truly believe something, it becomes your reality. If you disbelieve, it cannot manifest.

So, imagine what would happen if you tried to manifest physical well-being but don't believe that you deserve to be healed – or simply don't believe that the healing will take place at all. Your disbelief will act as a "gatekeeper" that will not allow your desire to manifest.

Even worse is that many of your beliefs are subconscious; you don't even know they are there. This can set you up to experience one of the more common problems we'll be discussing in a moment: conflicting desires. Conflicting desires occur when you consciously want something but subconsciously part of you resists it and will not allow it to manifest.

A good example is when you desperately want a better job, or to start your own business, but deep inside you fear that you may not have what it takes to be successful. This belief that you don't have what it takes will cause you to sabotage your efforts and block the manifestation.

Later in this guide we'll be exploring some good techniques for resolving conflicting desires.

## The Manifestation Process, In a Nutshell

Let's put all of the components together so you can see how they work.

When you think about something consistently, you start attracting it into your life. As you keep thinking about it, corresponding feelings are triggered, which boosts the intensity of your "request" – whether positive or negative. Then the universe responds by sending you more of the thing(s) you are focusing on, and if your belief system allows it, they will manifest.

*Blockages That Can Stand in the Way*

As we covered earlier, there are some common mistakes that people often make that can prevent the manifestation process from working correctly. Here are a few of them.

## Lack of Clarity About What You REALLY Want

Very often you may set an intention to attract a specific object or set of circumstances without really being clear about **why** you want it. That might not seem like such a big deal, except that often the situation or object you think you want won't be enough to satisfy your true needs.

For example, you may believe that having a bigger income will make you feel satisfied with your job, when deep down inside you may actually be craving a greater sense of fulfillment in your work. (Sure, a bigger income wouldn't hurt either – but that may not be your true motivation.) If you attempt to manifest a better-paying job without focusing on the true essence of what you want, you will either manifest a higher-paying job that still leaves you feeling dissatisfied, or you might block the entire manifestation so nothing changes at all.

To get clear on the essence of what you really want, consider an object or situation and then ask yourself what it will DO for you. Why do you want it? How will it make you FEEL? That feeling is what you're really after.

Once you've identified that feeling, you'll be in a much better position to focus on what you're truly trying to accomplish, and dramatically improve your ability to attract it.

**Conflicting Desires**

As we covered in the introduction to the Law of Attraction, conflicting desires can be hard to identify because they are often caused by subconscious fears, limiting beliefs, childhood conditioning and unhealthy habits.

However, with a little bit of introspection, you can usually gain some clarity. A good way to start is by thinking about something that you're trying to attract right now, and then consider how you feel about it.

Does the idea of it excite you, or make you nervous? Maybe a little bit of both? Feelings of nervousness, uncertainty or fear are strong indicators that you're not "clear" on this desire – you have some resistance that is likely related to limiting beliefs.

Here's a good way to identify what they might be:

Make a list of your biggest goals and dreams. Then, for every item on that list, insert it into the first blank spot in the following statement:

"If I were to have _____, I'm afraid that _____."

In the second spot, write down some negative or unpleasant outcomes that could potentially happen as a result of manifesting your goal.

Examples: "If I were to have a healthy body, I'm afraid that other people would expect too much of me." "If I were to have financial freedom, I'm afraid that I might mismanage my money and lose it all." "If I were to have a loving relationship, I'm afraid that he might cheat on me and mess it all up again."

Each of these fears is likely related to a past painful experience, or a limiting belief, or even a fearful thought that seems irrational but might be the result of childhood conditioning or a resistance to leaving your comfort zone.

Dealing effectively with these limiting beliefs and fears is as easy as diffusing them of their power. Ask yourself these two questions for every fear you can identify:

### 1) How likely is it to happen?

More often than not, the things we fear happening are not likely to happen at all - unless we keep focusing on them and attract them, of course! But our subconscious mind doesn't reason these things out; it simply regurgitates the limiting beliefs and fears we have programmed into it (and others have programmed into it for us). If you take a closer look at some of these fears, you'll probably find that they have a slim-to-zero chance of happening.

## 2) Could you handle it if it did happen?

Another thing to consider is that you are probably grossly underestimating your own ability to cope with challenges. It's natural to want to avoid discomfort, but if you were to face it, you'd probably just deal with it and move on. No big deal!

If you will use this process to clear out all of your limiting beliefs, fears and resistance to the things you are trying to attract, you will empower yourself like you wouldn't believe – and dramatically improve your manifesting results in the process.

## Environmental Negativity

Another major problem occurs when you are trying desperately to manifest better life experiences but you are still faced with a lot of negative situations and people each day. You might have a stressful job, relationship turmoil or financial difficulty – and keeping a positive focus on what you want to manifest can be extremely trying at times. As hard as you try not to get sucked into the negativity, you may still find yourself reacting to it, and if you do it enough you will delay the arrival of your better circumstances.

To combat this, you may want to start practicing a few techniques that will continuously bring you back into a positive mind-set.

### 1) Daily meditation

Meditating for just 10 to 20 minutes a day can have a huge impact on your peace of mind. It can quiet your thoughts, relax your body and stabilize your emotions so that you don't feel so overwhelmed, even when you're in the midst of negativity.

Simply find a quiet place to be alone, sit quietly and breathe slowly and deeply. Try to quiet your mind as much as you can, release scattered thoughts and relax your body completely.

### 2) Visualize more positive circumstances

Even when you're currently facing negative circumstances, you can use the power of your imagination to begin turning them around in the heat of the moment. If your boss came into work in a terrible mood and you felt it affecting your own mood, you could say to yourself, "I can imagine what it would be like to have a boss that's in a good mood every day. My work environment would be pleasant if that were the case; we'd all be laughing and feeling good as we did our work . . ." Continue imagining all of the great details as if they were happening now, and generate the feelings to match them.

Over time, you should notice the negativity subsiding – but even before that happens, you'll definitely notice that you feel more positive regardless.

## 3) Gratitude and appreciation

Expressing gratitude and appreciation on a regular basis can instantly shift you out of a negative state and into a positive one. Even better, you can use this technique at any time. It doesn't matter if you are immediately facing a negative situation or not.

Simply pick one thing about your current situation (or any situation you are trying to improve) that you can appreciate or feel grateful for, and focus all of your attention on it. You may find it helpful to narrate it mentally or verbally like this: "Even though I'm struggling with this illness right now, I do appreciate the fact that it has taught me a lot about slowing down and taking it easy. I've always been a hard worker, and sometimes I've carried that habit too far and overdone it. I need to learn how to take better care of myself and I'm definitely learning the importance of that in a powerful way now. I wouldn't wish for illness, but I can see how it is really a blessing in some ways."

Go on like that for as long as you like, allowing the feeling of appreciation to flow through you as you do. Within minutes you should find that you feel much better.

You can also use this same technique when you start to feel stressed, frustrated or annoyed in your everyday life. Just think about one thing that you are grateful for and keep your focus on it for a few minutes. For example, if you are driving and another driver cuts you off, your first impulse might be to throw a few choice words and hand gestures in his direction, but that's only going to keep you mired in negativity.

Instead, you might say to yourself, "Well, that was definitely not a nice thing to do, but I'm not going to dwell on it today. Instead, I'm going to focus on that beautiful new car over there. I love the color; I can see myself driving something like that someday. I imagine that the interior is loaded with neat features and a great stereo system . . ." Keep going until you have successfully distracted yourself from what you don't want (rude drivers) and switched to focusing on something you do want (a new car, or anything positive you choose to focus on).

One great thing that using the Law of Attraction can teach you is how to truly master your own thoughts and feelings. Eventually you come to realize that it doesn't matter how much negativity you face, because you ALWAYS have control over what you focus on. And the more you focus on positive things, the more the negativity is going to keep fading and fading, until it's almost nonexistent.

**Noticing The Absence of Your Desire**

Another big blockage is created when you keep "looking" at your surroundings to see if your desire has manifested yet.

This one can be tricky to recognize, but it gets easier if you make it a habit to consistently focus only on what you want to see more of in your life.

As an example, let's say that you're trying to attract a better job. You've been applying for some great positions but you're not yet getting any calls for interviews. Every day when you check the mail, you hope to see a letter from a prospective employer. You wait for the telephone to ring and check your messages a dozen times a day, but still no calls.

And every time you "look" for a call or letter and don't see one, you are disappointed that they haven't come yet. This feeling of disappointment is one you want to avoid at all costs because it will continue to block the new opportunity from arriving.

Instead, you can try two other options:

### 1) EXPECT to see what you want to see.

Rather than feeling anxious or pessimistic when you go to check the mail or your phone messages, make it your **intention** to find good news waiting for you. Say to yourself, "I bet there will be a letter with good news waiting for me today." Or when you check your phone messages say, "I bet someone called me to set up an interview today." The more you do this, the more you will communicate your enthusiasm and BELIEF to the universe, and the more the universe will respond by sending what you expect to see. However, even if it doesn't work right away, it's important not to get disappointed or angry.

Just let it go and say, "That's okay, I know it's coming soon."

## 2) Detach from expectations and pretend you already have it.

Another option is to forget expectations altogether and instead adopt the mood and mind-set of someone who **already** has a great job. Think of it this way: if you did already have the great job you want, what kind of attitude would you have when you went to check the mail or your phone messages? You'd be relaxed, happy, and detached from any particular outcome, right?

Adopt that attitude now! Just keep saying to yourself, "I know the universe is working on it and the perfect outcome will be delivered in the perfect way and at the perfect time." Then let it go. This air of calm, positive detachment can work wonders in manifestation because you're not emitting negative emotions and blocking opportunities from arriving.

### Trying to Put Everything in Motion Yourself

Manifesting something with the Law of Attraction requires a slightly different approach than you may be used to. Like most people, you may have been taught that the only way to make something happen is to roll up your sleeves and work hard for it. But with the Law of Attraction, you want to first get the energy flowing, and then stay open to any inspired actions that come up as a result of that energy and intention.

It's not that taking action is a bad thing, because it isn't. But taking massive action and trying to force something to happen very often creates unnecessary problems and delays. Even more importantly, by trying to put everything in motion yourself, you are basically communicating a message of distrust and disbelief to the universe. You're saying, "I don't trust that the Law of Attraction will work for me, so I'm going to do it all by myself." As a result, not much will happen unless you do the work yourself.

Instead, a much better approach would be to first set your intention, get very clear on the essence of what you want, spend a few days thinking about it and imagining how great it would be to have it – and then wait and see if the universe inspires you with any ideas on how to receive it.

Sometimes you'll conceive a great idea almost immediately, while other times nothing much seems to happen at first. Be patient, however, and wait and see what happens. If no ideas or hunches come spontaneously, you may want to officially consult your inner guidance for insights – which leads us to the next common mistake.

**Neglecting Your Inner Guidance**

As you learn to master the Law of Attraction, your inner guidance will rapidly become your most valuable tool. No matter how many questions you have and what they might be, your inner wisdom already knows the answers – all you have to do is ask!

There are two basic ways to use your inner guidance:

## 1) General Daily Guidance

It's a good idea to get into the habit of spending a few minutes each day tuning into your inner self and paying attention to any insights you seem to receive. If you begin meditating daily as we covered previously, this would be a great addition to that practice.

Simply sit quietly, turn your attention within and ask your inner self if there is anything you need to know right now, any avenues you should explore, and so on. Then wait quietly and see if anything pops into your mind, or if you get any feelings or hunches.

If not, don't worry about it and just check in again the next day. If so, write them down and give them some more thought. You might be given a great idea to help you achieve one of your goals, or create a healthier lifestyle, or simply feel happier.

## 2) Specific Insights and/or Inspired Action Ideas

You can also use your inner guidance when you're trying to make a decision or to receive inspired action ideas like we just covered in the last section.

Write down a question that you would like answered, such as, "How can I begin to attract more income?" "What can I do to improve my health?" "Is there anything I can do to speed the arrival of my dream home?"

You can even ask open-ended questions like this: "What do I need to know about my relationship with Mark?" "What am I missing when it comes to creating my dream career?"

Then wait quietly for a few minutes, remaining open to any insights you may receive. If none come immediately, don't despair. Very often ideas will pop into your mind spontaneously while you're doing something else.

## Refusing to Let Go and Trust

Just as rushing out to try and take care of everything on your own communicates a strong message of distrust to the universe, so does remaining emotionally attached to your desired outcome. By "emotionally attached" I mean constantly obsessing about it, worrying about whether it's on the way, and otherwise dwelling on it. Every time you do this, you only delay it further.

Also problematic is trying to control "how" your desire will manifest. It is not up to you to figure out the finer details of what form it takes and how it shows up – your job is to focus intently on the feeling you will experience when it arrives and let the universe take care of the rest.

Once again, this requires a certain measure of faith that the universe is working on your behalf, as well as faith in your own abilities as a deliberate creator, and faith that the Law of Attraction really works. It may take some time for you to build up to really believing these things.

However, you can start in small ways and before long you'll begin to gain momentum. Start by saying things like this to yourself, "I don't know how, but I do know that the universe is working on this manifestation for me. I have no idea how it will come, when it will come, or even what it will look like, but I'm willing to trust that it will be perfect in every way!"

The more you believe it, the more likely it is to be true.

**Holding Resistance in Your Body, Mind and Emotions**

Finally, one of the most common blockages people often experience when using the Law of Attraction is placing themselves in the wrong mental and emotional state to be able to receive what they've been asking for.

Remember at the beginning of this guide we covered the roles your thoughts, emotions and beliefs all play in the manifestation process? You cannot attract anything that is not in agreement with your current state of mind and emotion – which means that feelings like stress, frustration, jealousy, despair and anger should no longer be allowed to take up residence in your mind and body.

I'm not suggesting that you repress your emotions and become like a robot. Not only would that be impossible, it would be unhealthy even if you could do it. What you CAN do is learn to better manage your thoughts and emotions so that you end up focusing on the positive ones more often than you do the negative ones.

Every single day, your mission should be to let go of negative thoughts and feelings, and focus more and more on positive ones like these:

**Passion/Enthusiasm**

The more you can engage in activities that make you feel passionate and inspired, the more you are going to keep attracting situations that make you feel that way. As often as you can, spend time reading, viewing and doing things that make you feel great. Engage in some favorite hobbies, pursue new creative activities, dance and sing – the activities themselves aren't important, only your intention to do things that make you feel good.

**Peace and Tranquility**

Stress and tension are massive "resistance-generators" when it comes to the Law of Attraction. While it's not possible to completely eradicate stress from your life, you can do a lot to reduce and manage it on a daily basis.

Take time to do things that make you feel more relaxed, such as meditation, taking soothing baths, walking or sitting quietly in nature, or even taking regular catnaps. The more relaxed and happy you feel, the more easily your desires can manifest.

**Optimism**

Many people these days develop a chronic pessimistic outlook that can have a dramatic negative impact on their ability to manifest better circumstances. If this describes you, begin working to transform your pessimism into optimism.

You don't have to transform yourself into a "Pollyanna," but you can certainly begin deliberately choosing to expect the best and focus on the positive side of most situations in your life. When you do, you immediately start releasing the resistance in your energy signal and allowing better experiences into your life.

## Conclusion – Keep Going…

If there is one thing you take away from this book, let it be this …

No matter how far away you may feel you are from the realization of your desires, you should know that, from an *energetic* standpoint, you're probably a lot closer than you think. From the moment you decide you want something, things are in motion to make it happen for you.

Rather than getting caught up in taking external action, your main focus should be to envision your goal as though it already exists in the present. As you are doing this, know that there is a lot of "behind-the-scenes" movement going on, helping you in every way possible, but much of this movement will not be apparent to you.

In other words, know that once you establish your intention, your main objective is to live "as if" and not worry about the "how."

Stay aware and you will see signs along your path. These will confirm that you are on the right track.

Then simply keep working at it little by little, gradually improving your focus, adjusting your beliefs, and allowing more and more of the things you want into your life.

One more thing …

There is no such thing as luck, at least in the traditional definition. The "good" we attract is as direct result to the "good" we put out.

And now that you know that, go get lucky …

*Also Available from BoldThoughts.com:*

## DAVID HOOPER

# ASK, BELIEVE, RECEIVE

7 Days to Increased Wealth, Better Relationships, and a Life You Love (...Even When it Seems Impossible)

*David Hooper*

# the RICH SWITCH

The *Simple* 3-Step System To
**TURN ON INSTANT WEALTH**
Using the Law of Attraction